The Unarmed Truth

"Jon Sherwood dares to confront our 'empire' notions of faith and return us to the hard work of peacemaking. For too long, a wider culture of violence has edited and shaped the gospel to fit the convenience of retaliation, retribution, and revenge. Sherwood's work unmasks these false notions and places us on the path of communal restoration."

—**Otis Moss III**, professor of homiletics at the McAfee School of Theology at Mercer University

"An exciting book, reflecting a fresh discovery of Jesus-based nonviolence from an author with a most unlikely starting point. *The Unarmed Truth* demonstrates the continuing appeal of the radical way of Jesus."

—**David P. Gushee**, Distinguished University Professor of Christian Ethics at Mercer University

"One of the rarest things in our time is a person who has changed their mind. Even rarer is one who has truly changed their life. Sherwood has done both. He models repentance as the early church taught it, a radical reorientation of mind and life that comes from acknowledging Jesus' lordship in everything."

—**Meghan Larissa Good**, resource development manager of Jesus Collective and author of *Divine Gravity: Sparking a Movement to Recover a Better Christian Story*

"Gandhi considered Jesus the greatest person of nonviolence in history but lamented that the only people who don't know that Jesus is nonviolent are Christians.

Pastor John Sherwood walks us through the unarmed truth that Jesus was totally nonviolent, confronted systemic injustice head-on, and calls his followers to put down our weapons, renounce warfare, embrace his way of active, loving nonviolence, and go forth as peacemakers to announce the coming of God's reign of universal love and peace, a new world without violence, injustice, or war. May this little book inspire you to pursue the unarmed, disarming, nonviolent Jesus all over again and join his grassroots movement of gospel nonviolence."

—**Rev. John Dear**, longtime peace activist, Nobel Peace Prize nominee, director of BeatitudesCenter.org, and author of *Disarming the Heart*, *The Gospel of Peace*, and *Universal Love: Surrendering to the God of Peace*

"*The Unarmed Truth* is a courageous and timely call to rediscover Jesus as the Prince of Peace in a world addicted to violence—a mindset that has profoundly shaped even sincere Bible believers. Drawing from his own unlikely journey and writing with disarming honesty, Sherwood invites readers to grapple seriously with Scripture and to embrace the radical, enemy-loving way of the cross. *The Unarmed Truth* both challenges and inspires, calling us to a deeper, more faithful allegiance to the peaceable kingdom of Christ.

I warmly and wholeheartedly recommend this book to all who are serious about our Lord's command to love our enemies."

—**Douglas Jacoby**, international Bible teacher at International Bible Teaching Ministries

"A powerful and personal exploration of Jesus' call to nonviolence. In an age of unparalleled violence often justified in the name of Christianity, Sherwood presents a biblical framework for understanding the way of Jesus that critiques the notion of Christian nationalism and convincingly advocates for the peaceful use of nonresistance to affect societal transformation. I heartily endorse it for any Christian or congregation that wants to honestly explore the biblical, theological, and historical implications of the teachings of Jesus for our day."

—**Robert Nash**, professor emeritus of New Testament at Mercer University

The Unarmed Truth

Following the Prince of Peace in a World of Violence

Jon Sherwood

HERALD PRESS
Harrisonburg, Virginia

Herald Press
PO Box 866, Harrisonburg, Virginia 22803
www.HeraldPress.com

Library of Congress Cataloging-in-Publication Data
Names: Sherwood, Jon (Pastor) author
Title: The unarmed truth : following the Prince of Peace in a world of violence / Jon Sherwood.
Description: Harrisonburg, Virginia : Herald Press, [2026] | Includes bibliographical references.
Identifiers: LCCN 2026015785 (print) | LCCN 2026015786 (ebook) | ISBN 9781513817033 paperback | ISBN 9781513817040 ebook
Subjects: LCSH: Nonviolence—Religious aspects—Christianity | Nonviolence—Biblical teaching | Violence—Religious aspects—Christianity | Violence—Biblical teaching | Peace—Religious aspects—Christianity | Peace—Biblical teaching | BISAC: SOCIAL SCIENCE / Violence in Society
Classification: LCC BT736.6 .S48 2026 (print) | LCC BT736.6 (ebook)
LC record available at https://lccn.loc.gov/2026015785
LC ebook record available at https://lccn.loc.gov/2026015786

Study guides are available for many Herald Press titles at www.HeraldPress.com.

THE UNARMED TRUTH

Library of Congress Control Number: 2026015785
International Standard Book Number: 978-1-5138-1703-3 (paperback); 978-1-5138-1704-0 (ebook)
Printed in United States of America
Cover and interior design by Merrill Miller

Chapter 1 of this book includes discussion of suicide. If you or someone you know needs help, the national suicide and crisis lifeline in both Canada and the United States is available by calling or texting 988. In the United States, there is also an online chat at 988lifeline.org. In Canada, help is also available through Kids Help Phone (1-800-668-6868) and the Hope for Wellness Helpline (1-855-242-3310).

30 29 28 27 26 10 9 8 7 6 5 4 3 2 1

To my wife and children, my faith community,
and all those who would dare to believe
that the unarmed truth and unconditional love
will have the final word in reality.

Contents

Foreword

When I wrote a book arguing that race and racism are more about greed than they are about hate, I expected people to get upset about my critique of capitalism. But that was not in fact what made Christians most upset. What made them most upset was my claim, that I make alongside Jon Sherwood, the apostles, Christ, and the early church, that if we want to build communities of deep economic solidarity, it will require us to also be communities of creative antiviolence, as violence is definitionally the refusal to love and materially care for even one's enemies. If there is one way to make somebody mad, apparently all you need to do is say that we shouldn't ever kill one another.

The Unarmed Truth might make you upset. What Sherwood does in this book, however, is something that we all say we want: he points us to Christ and the people gathered by his Spirit in the church. Sherwood points us directly, accessibly, and uncompromisingly to our beautiful Savior and his way, reminding us that, among other things, Jesus Christ, the Son of God, calls his people clearly and unequivocally to lives of nonviolence.

I have hoped for a while to have a book that I can easily put in the hands of the Christian who is looking to figure out what Christian nonviolence looks like in a bloodthirsty land. Sherwood has given us that gift: one that calls each of us to Christlikeness, which is indeed the only thing that matters.

We are told by the author of Hebrews to fix our eyes on Christ, the pioneer and perfecter of our faith, who, for the joy set before him, endured the cross and despised the shame. If Christ is the first, we must follow him. We are to take up our crosses daily. One of those crosses is being a people who refuse to kill in a world that continues to try to convince us that killing is how we solve the world's problems. Sherwood will address many of your most visceral reactions. After all, he felt them just as you do. But he returns again and again to the life in Christ: if we are to be a people united mystically to the Son of God, at the very least, it must mean that we trust him to know what is best for us. In this way, our witness as the body of Christ is in our distinctiveness. How are we in but not of the world? By being a people who are unapologetically peacemakers in a world of warmakers.

Dear reader, I hope you are ready for what you will encounter in this book. I encourage you to continue to read only if you are really interested in living a life of obedience to Jesus Christ, a life of trust in his Spirit, and a life of love of his Father and those who bear God's image. If that is you, sister or brother, treasure this gift. And may it, like the goodness of God, guide us each to repentance and reconciliation with God and with one another!

—Rev. Malcom Foley
Special advisor to the president for campus engagement at Baylor University and author of *The Anti-Greed Gospel: Why the Love of Money Is the Root of Racism and How the Church Can Create a New Way Forward*

Preface

This book is born out of the desire to help more Christians see Jesus, and follow him, as the Prince of Peace. But this was not always my understanding of Jesus. I did not grow up in a context or Christian environment that saw Jesus as nonviolent. But when I became a Jesus follower in my early twenties and began seriously reading the Bible for myself, I started down a path that led to a changed heart and life, now including the writing of this book some twenty-five years later.

I wrote this book for people like me. People who love Jesus and his word. People who want to love their neighbor and positively contribute to the world. For those people, like me, who haven't heard much about Christian nonviolence and its centrality to discipleship to Jesus. If this is your first time engaging with Christian nonviolence explicitly, I encourage you to journey with an open heart and mind while examining the Scriptures to see if any of this is true (Acts 17:11).

This book did not come about in a vacuum. Much of the impetus for this book was born out of my years of pastoral ministry in the American South, and uniquely through a church that I help pastor in North Carolina that joined me on a courageous and audacious journey of viewing Jesus as nonviolent when we hadn't before. This journey also coincided with my doctor of ministry degree in justice and peacemaking at Mercer University in Atlanta, Georgia—home of Martin Luther King Jr., whose leadership in the United States civil rights movement was guided by convictions of Christian nonviolence.

I am not treading any new theological ground, and this book barely scratches the surface of areas normally engaged by scholars. Instead, this book invites everyday Christians to intentionally examine areas of their faith, culture, and implicit beliefs. In this book I present a well-worn path of the nonviolence of Christian discipleship—but I do this especially for those who have never known nonviolence as part of Christian discipleship.[1] For some, my scholarship may seem amateurish, to others it may feel dense, but my hope is that my experience, and that of our congregation, may serve as a path forward for the swaths of Christians, particularly in the United States, but also in Canada and around the globe, who are completely unfamiliar with Christian nonviolence.

This book sketches two thousand years of church history around the issues of violence and the sanctity of life. Jesus ushered in a nonviolent revolution through his life, death, and resurrection that, frankly, the church has struggled to be faithful to for much of that history. Because some, if not many, of my readers may be new to this subject, I have included sections on common questions about Christian nonviolence, both scriptural and ethical, that I have encountered along the journey. For ease of reference, those appear in the back of the book.

I am convinced there are lots of Christians out there just like me, just like the people in our congregation—and you may be one of them—who, given the opportunity, will come to understand, believe, and follow Jesus as the Prince of Peace. Jesus, who didn't overcome death through violence, but inaugurated a third way of peace through a cross-shaped reality of self-sacrificing love, calls us to follow him.

In and through Jesus, may it be so.

ONE

A War on Mars

A Southern Pastor's (Reluctant) Journey into Nonviolence

I want to invite you on a journey. This journey won't be easy, but like every good journey, it has an incredibly rewarding destination. One filled with peace and hope. A reality not marked with violence and vengeance, but one of peace and freedom, even from death. I invite you to journey alongside me and our church congregation—a journey taken in the American South.

I was born and raised in the South. I live in perhaps the most prosperous and militaristically powerful civilization to have ever existed in the world, the United States of America—a nation that advocates providing more freedoms and opportunities to its citizens than any other. It is arguably one of the most influential civilizations on the planet, exporting its cultural values across the world, and I have personally found myself at the epicenter of the historic societal and cultural power in America.

But all this power is from Mars.

For most of us Mars is the red planet, fourth from the sun, that can occasionally be seen with the naked eye. It tends to conjure up notions of science fiction and alien invasions, or perhaps future human colonization. However, in Jesus' day, Mars was the Roman god of war and the most important god in the pantheon after Jupiter. Mars represented warfare and the blessings of gods to vanquish enemies through might, domination, and bloodshed. Mars represented military power to secure peace, the Pax Romana, and was believed to be the father of the Roman people. It is in this context that Jesus, whom Isaiah prophesied was the Prince of Peace (Isaiah 9:6), introduced a new and radical way toward peace.

Jesus waged war against war itself by triumphing over death and the principalities of evil, not through military power but through his self-giving, sacrificial love of enemies—laying down his life for them. Instead of riding into Jerusalem to set God's people free from their occupiers on a military horse with a band of warriors armed to the teeth, Jesus rode in, unarmed and weeping, on a young donkey. He wept because he said they couldn't recognize what would bring them true peace but instead would only experience more violence and destruction. "If you, even you, had only known on this day what would bring you peace—but now it is hidden from your eyes. The days will come upon you when your enemies will build an embankment against you and encircle you and hem you in on every side. They will dash you to the ground, you and the children within your walls. They will not leave one stone on another, because you did not recognize the time of God's coming to you" (Luke 19:41–44).

I grew up here on Mars, probably like you did.

You know the place, with gun racks in pickup truck windows and American flags flying in front of churches. The place where *pacifist* is a curse word—equal with sedition.

I'm writing this book for us.

I was raised to be an American Christian—not a Muslim, Buddhist, or Hindu. I was raised believing in the god of war, and his name was Jesus. The Jesus who was a conquering warrior riding on a white horse, you know, a man's man who takes no prisoners and wages holy war.[1] I wasn't raised to be a pacifist—and I'm not Mennonite, Amish, Quaker, or Anabaptist. And I'm not Canadian. I'm a red-blooded southern American white man, born outside Atlanta in Decatur, Georgia, who was taught to never start fights, but to *always* finish them.

I was taught to shoot and care for guns before I could read and write well. I remember growing up in rural North Florida as a young boy just below the Georgia state line and playing in my grandfather's field with his US Army–issued mock M16 training rifle. It was a nonoperational, official weight, size, and shape training replica of the M16 rifle of that era. I was about six years old.

The South got somethin' to say

I want to warn you that over the next few paragraphs I share about drug use and suicidal ideation.

As a teenager I grew up on '90s southern hip-hop like Outkast, Goodie Mob, and Master P, and I echo the sentiments of rap legend André from Outkast, along with theologian Esau McCaulley, that on the subject of Christian nonviolence, "the South got somethin' to say."[2] As a latchkey kid in the South, I was inundated in the era of Rambo, *Top Gun*, MTV, and BET that taught me what it meant to be an American man: a man who would always see himself as the "good guy" in the story while blasting the enemy into smithereens. I was taught that enemies often didn't look like me either—they had different skin, hair, and dialect, and usually didn't believe in Jesus. At least not the Jesus I believed in. I was taught to be an American hero who would be ready to employ violence to bring about "peace," all in the name of Jesus. I was taught to be a sheep dog, a man who was not effeminate but instead was a protector for myself, my family, my community, and perhaps most especially, my country.

In her insightful book *Jesus and John Wayne: How White Christian Evangelicals Corrupted a Faith and Fractured a Nation,* history professor Kristin Kobes Du Mez says, "More than any other religious demographic in America, white evangelical Protestants support preemptive war, condone the use of torture, and favor the death penalty. They are more likely than members of other faith groups to own a gun, to believe citizens should be allowed to carry guns in most places, and to feel safer with a firearm around."[3] Perhaps this is partly why I was prone to violence during my teenage and young adult life.

I had an abusive relationship with my stepfather during my teen years and was often in violent situations while involved in the drug culture as a young adult. I came from a military family on both sides and nearly shipped out to Parris Island to become a US Marine when I was eighteen years old but ultimately didn't because of my drug addictions.[4] I trained as an amateur cage fighter and regularly carried an illegal firearm.

In hindsight, I was shaped to think and look more like a Spartan than a Christian. I grew up in what I would call a culturally Christian environment. The kind where Grandma would take us to church sometimes, but generally there wasn't a strong sense of God, the Scriptures, or faith permeating the home. There wasn't much prayer, Bible reading, or discussion about God or Jesus and the impact of our faith on our lives. But everyone considered themselves Christian. As an example of this cultural Christianity, I had a friend in high school who professed to love Jesus, and then would proceed to get high with me and take me to the youth group worship service *he led* so we could pick up girls.

By the time I was a late teen I had completely written off the Bible and Christianity as a hoax, a hypocritical facade. The church was a place for grandmas to be social, a place for the youth to gather and sin, but not a place of genuine spiritual inquiry, power, or change. I know this does not characterize every person's experience, nor every community of Christians, but unfortunately it is far too common.

It was in this context that I found myself turning to drugs and a life of hedonism and sin as I tried to navigate life. However, I had spiritual longings and often considered the big questions of life, such as, "What happens when I die?" "What is the meaning and purpose to my life?" and "Is there anything beyond what I can see—is there a spiritual reality?" As I longed for answers to these questions, I consistently found none.

I spoke to other people—my contemporaries, professors, friends, and family—anyone I could. I read and dabbled in Eastern religious thought as well as ancient and modern philosophies, but I wouldn't pick up the Bible (except occasionally to tear pages out in hotel rooms to roll joints of marijuana). I don't know if I had an aversion to reading the Bible because of the hypocrisy that I experienced in the name of Jesus, or if it was because I had some notion that the Bible was simply a human creation intended to domesticate people into upstanding citizens of an orderly society, but I believed there were no answers to be found there.

After battling depression and suicidal ideation for some time, I sat up one night while on drugs and contemplated suicide with a loaded gun in my hand. As I worked through every angle and detail that I could in my mind, the possibility of ending my life had been made much easier through the easy access I had to owning a gun. As bad as life had turned out for me, as hopeless and desperate as I had become, I thought there was a possibility it could get worse if I ended my life. This unknown possibility, some reality beyond death that could be *worse* than the life I was experiencing, ultimately led me to not pull the trigger that night.

Simply put, I was scared to die.

After that night I resolved that I would suffer the hopelessness and meaningless of life, but the spiritual longing inside me remained. During this season, through a series of providential events, I picked up the Bible for myself and started to read it, thinking I had nothing to lose—because I didn't.

The Jesus I never knew

I had heard the basic Christian narrative before—that Jesus died for my sins so that I could have eternal life. I had seen lots of John 3:16 signs held up at football games. When I was young, I said a prayer and invited Jesus into my heart with as much sincerity as I could muster. Yet I had never experienced any power or change in my life.

Don't get me wrong, I'm grateful for the positive faith experiences God orchestrated in my youth, and the faithful people he allowed me to encounter. And yet, I still ended up in a place of desperation and wanting to end my own life.

Not long after that night, God allowed me to meet a student on the campus of the community college where I had enrolled after dropping out of my first attempt at college.

He told me about a Jesus I had never heard of.

He introduced me to a Jesus who claimed he was *Lord*. Master. Ruler. King.

I had long heard of Jesus the *Savior*. The one who forgave my sins and gave me eternal life after I die (albeit in some blissful "heaven" that was ill-defined). I heard of the get-out-of-hell-free card I got from Jesus if I accepted him in my heart. But as I read the Bible with this college colleague, I realized there was a Jesus I had never heard of.

The Jesus of the *Scriptures*.

The Jesus who said if I was going to follow him, I had to take up my cross and deny myself (Luke 9:23). Who said I must love him more than everyone else, including my own family (Luke 8:21; 14:26–27)! The Jesus who said he would spit me out of his mouth if I was lukewarm and unwilling to repent (Revelation 3:16). The Jesus who said I must have an attitude that is willing to gouge out my eye and cut off my hand if they cause me to sin (Matthew 5:27–30)!

This Jesus hit different.

And this Jesus was being proclaimed to me through the Scriptures by a young man who said he and his girlfriend of three years had never even kissed, much less had sex, because of their devotion to Jesus as *both* Lord and Savior!

I was baffled—and *enthralled*.

Could this Jesus empower me to live a life I couldn't on my own? Could this Jesus provide meaning and purpose for me in ways nothing else in life could? Could this Jesus be the way?

With the combination of the Scriptures and an authentic life of witness, I knew I had a decision to make. I had to decide what I thought of *this* Jesus. I had to come to grips with the fact that I had dismissed Jesus and the Bible because of other Christians, not because of *Jesus*. I was humbled, and I was grateful. Grateful that God hadn't given up on me but had seen me in my distress and pulled me out of my pit of darkness (Psalm 31:9; 1 Peter 2:9), and showed me the meaning of life in the person and words of Jesus (Matthew 4:19; 11:28; 28:18–20; John 5:24; 8:31–32).

It was at this point that my life radically changed. God enabled me to overcome addictions, reconcile relationships—including with my abusive stepfather—and make radical decisions to implement change in my life. I also entered a community of brothers and sisters in the Lord. I experienced joy and peace like I had never known. I cried a lot—and I asked for forgiveness from those I had wronged. I went on a repentance rampage and burned my drug paraphernalia and pornography. I was no longer afraid to die—and lived like never before.

I later asked a relative who had known me before becoming a Christian what they thought happened to me when my life radically changed. They said they had no idea, because they were sure I would end up dead or in jail.

I told them it was the *power of God.*

Not long after becoming a Christian I graduated from college and devoted myself to the calling and work of vocational ministry. For over a decade I was a college pastor in several churches and ministered to college students throughout the South in Florida, Alabama, Georgia, and South Carolina before becoming the lead pastor of a congregation in North Carolina.

Many Christians in America today don't question following Jesus onto the field of battle to kill their enemies. Most Christians I encounter feel fine owning firearms for self-defense from their enemies. And yet they have rarely considered what Jesus' teachings on nonviolence and nonretaliation might mean for their worldview and practices surrounding gun ownership. Many Christian pulpits and podcasts are devoid of the nonviolent teachings of Jesus and their implications. I know in my own faith journey I heard very little about nonviolence explicitly.

Early on in my faith, through a cursory reading of the Gospels, I understood that Jesus wanted me to give up my violent life and didn't want me to kill other people, whom he had also died for. Perhaps this was because of my particularly violent past, one that made me more sensitive to the topic as I walked with Jesus. In my first several years of following Jesus, I prayed constantly that God wouldn't allow anyone to be confrontational with me, because I didn't believe I would have the self-control to not respond violently. Thankfully, he answered my prayers and never allowed me to be tempted beyond what I could bear (1 Corinthians 10:13).[5]

One of the first memories I have of interacting directly with Christian nonviolence theology in a pastoral setting was a conversation with my roommate about keeping a loaded gun in the house. The year prior, through the power and aid of the Holy Spirit, I helped him become a follower of Jesus. He was an ex–gang member from Los Angeles who had fled gang life and ended up in the Atlanta suburbs, where I was a college pastor. After he became a Christian, we became roommates, and he warned me not to enter the house loudly during the night. Otherwise, he might mistake me for someone else and shoot me with the loaded snub-nosed .38 caliber pistol he slept with under his pillow. He had this pistol ready because he still feared for his life after leaving the gang.

At the time I still owned a handgun. I kept it unloaded and locked in the house but had developed the conviction that I would not shoot another person with it.[6] This led me to discuss my convictions around the nonviolent and peacemaking teachings of Jesus with my roommate more thoroughly, and to consider whether, as a follower of Jesus, he felt comfortable killing someone for any reason. I considered the conversation successful at the time, as he told me he would at least move the loaded gun from under his pillow to his bedroom closest.

As a college pastor these kinds of private conversations would happen occasionally, particularly with other young men. This was especially the case as young men considered entering the US military as a career path—many times because they felt as though they had no other viable upward options for their life. Inevitably in these conversations I would bring Christian nonviolence to their attention and ask them to consider Jesus' life and teachings seriously before making this kind of decision. That conversation was *always* the first time they had ever heard of such things, much less been challenged to seriously consider them—even for those who had grown up in church. As I continued to discuss the nonviolent nature of the gospel with others, I became increasingly aware of how strange these teachings were—and yet as we discussed, prayed, and wrestled with the Scriptures, greater clarity came as we saw Jesus to be the Prince of Peace.

My journey into the nonviolent way of Jesus didn't happen in isolation or only in one-on-one encounters. It developed over time and particularly unfurled alongside a small Southern church community I have the privilege of helping lead. During my doctoral studies in Atlanta, the church and I began an honest, uncomfortable, and ultimately transformative process of learning what it means to follow Jesus as the Prince of Peace.

During our journey of understanding Jesus in this manner, I witnessed several recurring threads, such as common objections to nonviolence, the deeply emotional nature of the subject, and certain cultural and social influences that we are entangled in. In this book I want to pull some of those threads as well as present the case for Jesus' nonviolent revolution that confronts our idolatry of power and violence. Jesus was radically nonviolent, and he calls his followers to be the same.

While this may be familiar territory to some, I am especially writing to those that have not heard much about this before in the church. As was the case with our congregation, people must understand how we got here in order to understand how to get somewhere else. So my approach here is largely chronological, beginning with Jesus and the New Testament,[7] tracing Christian approaches to nonviolence throughout church history, and ending with current cultural contexts while painting a way forward and discussing the specifics of our church's journey. In this book I seek to address questions such as the following:

1. *What does the New Testament have to say?* Providing the scriptural witness for nonviolence as seen in the life and ministry of Jesus and his followers.

2. *How has the church dealt with nonviolence historically?* A high-level overview of nonviolence in the history of the Christian church.

3. *How did we get here?* A look at contemporary considerations of nonviolence and proposals for ways forward in Jesus' peaceable kingdom while living in a world of violence.

At the back of the book, you'll find responses to common scriptural and ethical questions that I've frequently heard from those encountering Christian nonviolence for the first time.

As a congregation, we have experienced incredible change on our journey as the Spirit of God has led to members disarming, loving their enemies practically while in the face of threat, and living as outposts of peace and beacons of hope in the world.

I hope this book will invite you to do the same.

My personal journey has been fraught with difficulty as I have tried to take a stand for my convictions around Christian nonviolence. Even among family members, close Christian friends, and other pastors I have been misunderstood, scoffed at, dismissed, canceled, and jeered at. My conviction is certainly not convenient, nor is it popular. However, this all pales in comparison to my Lord and his followers through the centuries who have paid with their own lives before they would respond or retaliate violently against another.

I seek to take up that prophetic witness, that bloodstained banner, and proclaim Jesus as a king of a nonviolent and revolutionary kingdom. A kingdom that bids us to love our enemies and pray for those who persecute us (Matthew 5:44). But this is incredibly difficult. We are all shaped by our contexts and cultures. Christians throughout history have struggled to integrate their faith into their cultural realities and have struggled to love enemies while at the same time loving their neighbors. But we must wrestle together to examine our cultural biases and pray that God will reveal our blinders, shining light into the dark places where we have accepted beliefs and practices that are not representative of his kingdom.

If I'm honest, though, I am a reluctant prophetic witness. At times a reluctant pacifist. I would be lying if I said it hasn't been agonizing to be looked at weirdly or thought of as a crazy person by my family, peers, and even other pastors as I proclaim the nonviolent ways of Jesus. Like the apostle Paul, I am a violent man who was shown mercy, though at one time I acted in ignorance and unbelief (1 Timothy 1:13). Jesus calls us to follow him, the Prince of Peace, on a narrow road while proclaiming the unarmed truth and experiencing a truly flourishing human life—one marked by nonviolence.

TWO

But I Tell You

Jesus' Vision of Enemy Love

Jesus was a revolutionary, and the Jewish people were desperate for a revolution.

For centuries they had been subjugated by foreign powers: the Assyrians, the Babylonians, the Persians, the Greeks, and in Jesus' day, the Romans. Their identity, their temple, and their very lives had been shaped and reshaped under the shadow of dominating empires that had no respect for their God or their way of life. These empires were built on the foundations of violence and perpetuated through bloodshed. The Israelites were looking for someone to lead them out of captivity and out from under the oppressive rule of the Roman Empire. In Jesus' lifetime several messianic figures came on the scene to establish God's kingdom through violent revolution.[1]

Though there were many complex and nuanced views in Israel about the coming Messiah during the days of Jesus, the identifying feature of the truly faithful Israelite was whether they were willing to take up the sword against the oppressor of God's people.[2] The cries of the oppressed saturated the air, and violent oppression created a staggering resentment from the conquered, but beneath the surface of the Israelites' daily existence simmered a seed of hope—a longing waiting to blossom in the Messiah who would change everything, restoring their national and religious glory as in the days of Kings David and Solomon. The prophets had foretold of a king, the anointed one of God who would rule with justice and compassion (Isaiah 11).

The faithful clung to this hope despite the hopeless circumstances. It is what caused Simeon to poetically proclaim that he could die in peace because his eyes had seen the Lord's salvation in the baby Jesus, who would be the light of revelation to the Gentiles and the hope of glory for Israel (Luke 2:25–32).

But Jesus was a revolutionary unlike anyone was hoping for.

A Jesus-centered approach to Scripture

Before we look closer at Jesus or his revolution, we must take a moment to consider how we read and understand Scripture. André Trocmé, a French pastor famous for saving thousands of Jews from the Nazis during World War II, said, "Jesus *is* the central event of history, because de facto his coming changed humanity."[3]

For those of us who believe that Scripture is divinely inspired and has authority for our lives (2 Timothy 3:16; 2 Peter 1:21), it is proper to view all the Bible through the lens of Jesus—who himself said that all of Scripture points to him. Jesus said that when we look at him, we see God. In fact, he said it is possible for us to study the Scriptures diligently and yet miss them entirely if they don't point us to him (John 5:39–40). This method of understanding Scripture is what scholars call Christocentrism. In other words, God looks like Jesus.

Craig Bartholomew and Michael Goheen write in *The Drama of Scripture*, "According to the biblical narrative, the meaning of our whole world's history has been most fully shown to us in the person of Jesus."[4] This Jesus-centered way of reading Scripture is our lens for understanding all the diversity contained in the Bible.[5] In fact, this is how the New Testament authors themselves viewed the Hebrew Scriptures. Through the revelation of Jesus, the Son of God, they saw the fulfillment of all Scripture. In this perspective, the New Testament is an interpretation, or series of interpretations, of the Old Testament in the light of the person and work of Jesus.[6]

So when we consider ethical postures or actions as Christians, we must ask whether our ethics fit with Scripture as read through the prophetic lens of Jesus.[7] A fragmented reading of the Bible, rather than reading it as a unified story that leads to Jesus, may produce theologically orthodox, morally upright, warmly pious Christians—whose lives are more shaped by the idolatry of their cultural story than by Scripture.[8] As we read Scripture in this Jesus-centered way, we are wise to harmoniously employ tradition, direct divine guidance, church leadership, reason, science, experience, and what theologian Walter Brueggemann calls *prophetic imagination*—the ability to resist the triumphalism of Pharaoh in all its countless contemporary manifestations, and to energize the people of God to criticize the domineering empire, even in the face of profound grief.[9]

The Christians of the first few centuries CE viewed all of Scripture through this clarifying Christocentric lens of the person and life of Jesus. They trusted God's character as revealed in the crucified and risen Christ, even if those portraits seemed to conflict with or contradict earlier portraits of God in Scripture. They did this while at the same time continuing to faithfully affirm all Scripture as God-breathed (2 Timothy 3:16).[10] In his book on early Christian attitudes about war, George Kalantzis writes that "the Incarnation provided a new interpretive lens, a radical shift in history, and the juxtaposition in Matthew, 'you have heard it said . . . but I tell you' . . . was understood as a fulfillment of the law."[11] For today's disciples of Jesus, the cross and resurrection must provide the lens through which we see the world and the cruciform shape by which we are to exist in it.[12]

For the better part of one thousand seven hundred years, the church has debated the role of violence for Jesus' followers and his church, but this was not the case for the first three centuries. Though this debate is not new, Jesus is quite clear in his life and teachings on the issue, as were his earliest disciples and the authors of the New Testament. So were the members of the primitive church, who were unanimous in their understanding of Jesus' nonviolent kingdom for roughly two hundred fifty years after Christ's death and resurrection. In 2018, professor Terrence Rynne says that over the past fifty years, scholarship on the nonviolence of Jesus, and its relationship to the church, has widened and deepened—and it continues to pick up speed.[13]

Hallelujah!

The scriptural cornerstone of Christian nonviolence

Any discussion about Christian nonviolence must begin by looking seriously at Matthew 5:43–48. But before we look at the passage, we must define terms. Violence, and thus nonviolence, can be tricky to define. Violence can be defined in myriad ways, such as direct and indirect, physical and nonphysical, verbal and nonverbal, visible and invisible, individual and systemic, and many others. While I recognize these difficulties, I primarily have in view the *Oxford English Dictionary* definition: "The exercise of physical force so as to inflict injury on, or cause damage to, persons or property; action or conduct characterized by this; treatment or usage tending to cause bodily injury or forcibly interfering with personal freedom."[14]

Matthew 5:43–48 is the scriptural cornerstone for Jesus' ethic on nonviolence in the kingdom of God. Jesus' teaching of enemy love is contained within the Sermon on the Mount, the Magna Carta of his teachings presented by the eyewitness evangelist Matthew.

> You have heard that it was said, "Love your neighbor and hate your enemy." But I tell you, love your enemies and pray for those who persecute you, that you may be children of your Father in heaven. He causes his sun to rise on the evil and the good, and sends rain on the righteous and the unrighteous. If you love those who love you, what reward will you get? Are not even the tax collectors doing that? And if you greet only your own people, what are you doing more than others? Do not even pagans do that? Be perfect, therefore, as your heavenly Father is perfect. (Matthew 5:43–48)

Though people have likely debated the precise meaning of many of Jesus' words since they were uttered and written down, his teaching here is clear. His call to a radical ethic of loving our enemies was, and is, the highest calling known to humans.[15]

It is simply otherworldly.

But how can we love our enemies if they are threatening our lives or the lives of our loved ones? When we read Jesus' words, we think he says that we should love our enemies *up to a point.* It's hard to take Jesus at his word. Most Christians today believe that you can love your enemies even if you must kill them under certain circumstances.

As we focus on Jesus' nonviolent teachings, we must recognize that Matthew intends to form a community of believers who renounce violence as a means by which to exert its will.[16] When asked about the greatest commandment, Jesus replied that there are two: to love God and to love one's neighbor as oneself (Matthew 22:36–40). In the Sermon on the Mount, Jesus extends the call to love one's neighbor to include loving one's enemies.

This is a radical game changer.

Matthew situates this in the sermon as the culmination of what are known as the six antitheses.[17] Six times, Jesus contrasts and fulfills the law of Moses with his teaching: "You have heard it said, but I tell you." He contrasts murder and anger, adultery and lust, divorce and adultery, oaths and speaking truthfully, retribution and nonviolent resistance, and loving neighbors and enemies (Matthew 5:21–48). The sixth and final antithesis about loving one's enemies summarizes and envelops all the ethical teaching of the preceding five. It also radically reorients the popular human notion of only loving those inside our own groups.

We are so good at creating us-versus-them categories: Democrat and Republican, liberal and conservative, immigrant and citizen, Black and White, straight and queer, and on and on it goes.

Jesus says that even those thought to represent the very betrayal of God's kingdom—the Jewish tax collectors employed by Rome to extort their countrymen (see also John the Baptist's teaching in Luke 3:7–14)—love those who love them back! The gospel of Matthew frequently depicts Jesus scandalizing his pious audiences' understanding of love while profoundly exposing their bigotry, prejudice, and elitism. May we who call on the name of Jesus allow him to do the same for us today.

Jesus said that to love one's enemies is based on the love of the heavenly Father and is the very thing that causes us to be like him and associated with him. Jesus is not trying to frustrate us with an unachievable ideal. He is challenging us to grow in obedience to God's will, which is to love indiscriminately. Jesus says that the love of enemies is not based on some ethical ideal that exists in a vacuum; we are called to love our enemies simply because God loves his own enemies. Theologians call this God's *common grace*—the gracious favor God bestows commonly on everyone without distinction.[18]

God demonstrates his indiscriminate love by causing the sun to shine and the rain to fall equally on all people (Matthew 5:45). Jesus says that we are to become perfect by loving all people, just as God does. The word translated as "perfect" in the NIV (*teleios*) could be more appropriately translated as "mature," "whole," or "complete."[19] Jesus says our love for others, especially our enemies, is what it means for us to become whole and complete like God, who shows love to both the righteous and the unrighteous. Theologian N. T. Wright notes that "enemies of the state are not enemies of YHWH, and if Israel is really to imitate her heavenly father, she must learn to love them and pray for them."[20]

The command to love one's enemies is not to be seen as one demand among many, but rather the apex of all commands that lead to the perfection of God. Through his teaching on enemy love, Jesus is reshaping the well-known Shema prayer of the Torah from Deuteronomy 6:4–5—"Love the Lord your God with all your heart and with all your soul and with all your strength"—to show that we truly become like God when we believe that our neighbor *includes* our enemies. For Christians this effectively means that we no longer have enemies, because *everyone is our neighbor*. In this way, Jesus reenvisions and embodies the Hebrew Scriptures and the will of God for everyone.

In Matthew's gospel, the phrase "kingdom of heaven" can be read as "God's empire," because Matthew is situated in his Roman colonizer context and reveals a radically different way of being the faithful people of God. The people of God are not to inhabit God's kingdom the way those situated in the kingdom of Mars do, through violence and domination. Jesus says the way forward for Israel is not the way of violence but rather a different, more oblique way of creative nonviolent resistance. He reveals this oblique and creative way in the recurring refrain in the Sermon on the Mount: "You have heard it said, but I say to you." In the sermon, Jesus is literally reinterpreting the Scriptures—or perhaps embodying, fulfilling, and clarifying them if you prefer.[21] In the six antitheses of Jesus' Sermon on the Mount, he proclaims that God's reign will create a communal life for his followers marked by actions that embody Jesus' interpretations of God's will concerning murder, adultery, divorce, oaths, nonviolent resistance, and love for neighbors, which he defines to include enemies.

The people who heard Jesus utter these words, along with those after the gospel was penned, would have been very familiar with the teaching to love one's neighbor. Jesus was directly quoting Leviticus 19:18: "Do not seek revenge or bear a grudge against anyone among your people, but love your neighbor as yourself. I am the LORD." However, the words "hate your enemy" from Matthew 5:43 occur nowhere in the Hebrew

Bible. So why did Jesus say they had heard to hate their enemies? Where exactly had they heard this?

Kernels of enemy love and the prophetic rebukes of the idolization of militarism appear in texts throughout the Old Testament.[22] Scholars debate whether Jesus' reference to hating one's enemies is inferred from texts like Deuteronomy 7:2; 23:3–6; 25:17–19; 30:7; Psalms 26:5; or 139:21–22 (Deuteronomy 30:7, for example, says "The Lord your God will put all these curses on your enemies who hate and persecute you.") However, the Dead Sea Scrolls, dating from the third century BCE to the first century CE, explicitly teach hatred of those regarded as enemies based on these passages. In other words, neither Jesus' listeners nor Matthew's readers would have been surprised by the words "hate your enemy," since this interpretation was regularly associated with these texts. Generally, in the Jewish world of Jesus' day, *neighbor* meant fellow Jew, and *enemy* meant everyone else (the Gentiles).

The point could not be clearer: *To follow Jesus means to love everyone, even your enemies, because loving one's enemies is at the very heart of the identity of someone in the kingdom of heaven.*

Jesus' teaching on nonviolent resistance and enemy love in the Sermon on the Mount is the cornerstone of Jesus' kingdom ethic. As we'll explore next, Jesus embodied and lived out this ethic in a world ruled by violence. Jesus subversively confronted the power structures of the Roman Empire and fought against them in ways no one predicted. And he overcame its power through a victory no one would believe.

At least at first.

THREE

Subversive Confrontation

Jesus and the Powers

The Romans entered the political scene in Israel around 63 BCE during the internecine battle between the Hasmonean rivals, the successors of the Maccabees.[1] The Maccabees were Jewish rebel warriors who retook control of Judea and restored Jewish worship in Jerusalem. In this political and social context under Roman rule, there is no doubt that Jesus came to be seen as a revolutionary, but his revolution was nothing like people had envisioned. It was dangerous, and at the same time bewildering.

From the very beginning, there was something different about Jesus. Jesus didn't show up with a sword in his hand or a gang at his back. In Mark's account of Jesus' arrest, Jesus asks the Roman police why they have come to arrest him with weapons as though he was a "dangerous revolutionary" (Mark 14:48 NLT) or a "man inciting revolt" (NASB). Jesus didn't come as a revolutionary the way people had seen other revolutions, with weapons and violence. Instead, he came quietly, humbly, born in a manger, far from the palaces of power, and didn't invoke the world's might to accomplish his goal.

When Peter, one of Jesus' closest disciples and friends, draws a sword to try to protect him, Jesus says that he could call upon violent power to accomplish his goals, but that is not the way of the kingdom. "Put your sword back in its place," Jesus tells Peter, "for all who draw the sword will die by the sword. Do you think I cannot call on my Father, and he will at once put at my disposal more than twelve legions of angels? But how then would the Scriptures be fulfilled that say it must happen in this way?" (Matthew 26:52–54).

Instead of weapons and violence, Jesus came preaching repentance and revolutionary love. "'The time has come,' he said. 'The kingdom of God has come near. Repent and believe the good news!'" (Mark 1:15). "Love the Lord your God with all your heart and with all your soul and with all your mind. This is the first and greatest commandment" (Matthew 22:37–38). His followers were not soldiers (except for perhaps Simon the Zealot), but fishermen, tax collectors, and women of little status—ordinary people from society with no great power, prestige, or influence.

Jesus' message was radical, but it wasn't the rallying cry for violent rebellion that many had expected—or even hoped for. It wasn't about military might or political conquest; it was about repentance, love, forgiveness, and becoming a new creation family.

But Jesus was not killed for being loving, nice, and nonviolent.

Jesus was brutally murdered because he exposed the evil powers of the world, even those that invoked the name of God. He did this in the most audacious manner, calling out evil and wickedness, then absorbing the world's evil and wickedness through his own sacrificial love, overcoming death itself by his resurrection from the dead.

Jesus stood on the side of the weak and took up their cause (Luke 4:18; see also Isaiah 61:1). At times, he treated rulers and those who abused power harshly, but he was tender with the weak and vulnerable. He blessed children and gave them status in a context where they were invisible (Mark 10). When all others were calling for the death penalty, he did not condemn the woman caught in adultery as a sinful criminal (John 8). And he treated with dignity and compassion a woman who was drawing water in the heat of the day, an outcast in cultural status because of her checkered sexual and relational past (John 4).

Jesus resisted the power that could have been available to him: he did not give in to the temptations of false power from the evil one in the desert (Matthew 4), and he did not call upon the power of the heavenly hosts to rescue him from death (Matthew 26). As Franciscan friar Richard Rohr points out, even though the church has often succumbed to the temptations of violence, power politics, and militarism, Jesus chose the power of powerlessness.[2] Or in the words of the apostle Paul, Jesus "disarmed the powers and authorities, he made a public spectacle of them, triumphing over them by the cross" (Colossians 2:15).

Jesus was a king, but his kingdom was unlike any other (John 18:36). "The kingdom of God has come near," he said. "Repent and believe the good news" (Mark 1:15). People had heard words like these before, but never from someone who so defied their expectations. Many were waiting for a warrior-king, someone who would lead them into battle and make them a free nation-state once more—as in the times of Kings David and Solomon. But Jesus wasn't interested in leading them to victory over the empire of Rome. He was offering something far more powerful—and far more dangerous: victory, freedom, and power over sin and death itself.

"Blessed are the poor in spirit, for theirs is the kingdom of heaven," he proclaimed. "Blessed are those who mourn, for they will be comforted" (Matthew 5:3–4). His message wasn't one of power, but vulnerability. He wasn't telling people to fight for a crown; he told them to take up a cross. And when people tried to crown him king *by force*, he enigmatically evaded their plot and stayed focused on his mission (John 6:15).

Inevitably, people struggled to understand Jesus. I mean, how could they?

Even Jesus' closest students were constantly being rebuked for being so slow to understand. Everyone was desperate for a hero to ride in on a war horse, to rally them in the streets, to burn the Roman banners and restore Israel to glory. Instead of fulfilling their hopes, Jesus healed the sick, fed the hungry, performed miracles, and spoke in parables.

His was a kingdom not of armies, but of reconciliation, love, and peace. Even his closest followers couldn't see it at the time because they were caught up in their own dreams of glory. Two of his closest disciples, James and John, once asked him, "Let one of us sit at your right and the other at your left in your glory" (Mark 10:37). They couldn't yet grasp what kind of kingdom Jesus was establishing, as they were still thinking of power in terms of thrones and positions of authority, not sacrifice, service, and crosses. Jesus used the situation to explain what authority is like in his kingdom. The world exercises authority over others to get them to do what they want, but

Jesus testified that true authority and power come through the vehicles of service and voluntary enslavement to others (Mark 10:42–45).

No wonder Jesus told people the road to life was narrow, and few find it (Matthew 7:14).

When Jesus was arrested because he had enraged the powers of the world, his revolution seemingly fell apart. The one man who had dared to speak of peace and love was seized by the authorities. His disciples, those who had followed him with such hope and devotion, fled to save their own lives. The revolution they had imagined—a revolution of power and glory—had turned into something they didn't want at all: an *invitation to willingly die.*

But before they ran, Peter, the boldest of them all, did perhaps one of the most natural things anyone in that situation could have done. He attempted to defend his loved ones, his innocent Rabbi and Lord, and cut off someone's ear with a sword—and surely, he wasn't aiming for his ear (John 18:10). After Jesus rebuked Peter's attempt, the rest of the disciples scattered into the night, confused and afraid, unwilling to follow Jesus into the inevitable confrontation with the powers of violence and domination that would ultimately lead to his death.

But Jesus' revolution continued that night nonetheless.

Although Jesus didn't employ violence and coercion to establish his kingdom, he was confrontational and subversive to the kingdoms of the world. Jesus was not passive in his mission to establish God's kingdom. In fact, after Jesus was arrested and brought before Pontius Pilate, the Roman governor, Jesus told Pilate that the very differentiator between his kingdom and the one Pilate represented was that neither he nor his followers employed violence to establish it!

All the gospel witnesses reveal a Messiah in Jesus who is consistently nonviolent, but I want to take a closer look at this showdown with Pilate as depicted in the gospel of John because it is one of the starkest contrasts between the kingdom of God and the kingdoms of the world.

As told in John 18:28–19:16, the trial of Jesus before Pilate is a masterclass in irony. It's a story where the judge is terrified, the accusers are the lawbreakers, the guilty are acquitted, and the prisoner sent to execution is the only one who is truly free.

Pilate asks Jesus, "Are you the king of the Jews?" In his response, Jesus reveals how his kingdom differs from Pilate's in matters of power, truth, violence, and righteousness. This conflict of kingdoms begs the questions, *Who is truly king? Is there such a thing as truth? What is the role of violence?* And, *Who gets to decide what is right and wrong*?

On the morning after Jesus' arrest, the religious leaders take Jesus from the high priest to the Praetorium, the Roman governor's palace. The leaders refuse to enter the building because it would defile them, making them unable to eat the Passover meal. So Pilate—the powerful Roman prefect—is forced to play the part of a messenger, pacing back and forth between the religious elite outside and the silent prisoner inside. When Pilate asks for a formal charge, they offer none, simply saying, "If he were not a criminal, . . . we would not have handed him over to you" (18:30).

Pilate retreats inside to face Jesus. He is looking for a revolutionary, a threat to Rome, but he finds something much more unsettling. He asks, "Are you the king of the Jews?" (18:33). Jesus' response shifts the entire gravity of the room. He explains that his kingdom is not of the sort that uses worldly violence to survive. "My kingdom is not of this world. If it were, my servants would fight. . . . But now my kingdom is from another place" (18:36).

When Pilate asks if he is a king at all, Jesus identifies himself as a witness to the truth. Pilate, cynical and weary, scoffs with one of the most famous questions in history: "What is truth?" (18:38).

Pilate ultimately finds no guilt in Jesus and tries to use a Passover custom to release him, offering the crowd a choice between Jesus and a known insurrectionist named Barabbas. The crowd's rejection is visceral: "Give us Barabbas!" (18:40). Pilate then attempts a brutal compromise. He has Jesus flogged—a bloody, bone-deep scouring—and the soldiers mock him with a crown of thorns and a purple robe. Pilate brings the mangled, bleeding Jesus before the crowd, hoping for pity, but the crowd roars, "Crucify! Crucify!" (19:6).

Getting nowhere with the crowds, Pilate is bewildered by Jesus' silence amid the prefect's power to kill or free him. Pilate then grows afraid as the designation "Son of God" is laid at the feet of Jesus, and the religious leaders play their final card: they threaten Pilate's own career, claiming that if he lets Jesus go, Pilate is "no friend of Caesar" (19:12).

Pilate is stuck. In a final proclamation the religious leaders cry out, "We have no king but Caesar" (19:15)! The story ends not with a legal victory, but with the true King beginning his march toward the place called the Skull.

Who is truly king?

Let's take a closer look at the four key questions in the confrontation between Pilate and Jesus. John's narrative of this trial reveals who really has power, who is truly king, and who ultimately controls life and death. Of course, Pilate thinks it is him. His understanding, which represents all human understanding, their kingdoms, and their wisdom, is that he has power over Jesus because he can kill him. Pilate has the soldiers, he has the weaponry, he has the money and the backing of the state. He is in control.

But Jesus bewilders and upends him.

Pilate is shocked when Jesus won't respond to defend his life (John 19:10). Jesus confounds Pilate's assumptions by saying that any power Pilate possesses over him is ultimately from God. This surprises and scares Pilate, and from then on, he tries to free Jesus—as he apparently comes to believe that Jesus truly is a king (vv. 14–15). It is a natural reaction to fear and be bewildered by those who are not afraid to die, especially those who are willing to lay down their lives voluntarily. But this is the power that faith in Jesus and the resurrection are *supposed* to produce in us, as we are freed from the fear of death that has enslaved us all our lives (Hebrews 2:14–15).

Is there such a thing as truth?

In Jesus' and Pilate's clash over who controls life and death, another dispute emerges about the nature of reality and truth itself. Jesus makes a bold statement—not only *is* there such a thing as truth; his very existence *testifies to it.* Jesus says that all who would side with truth will listen to his testimony about God. This is one of many clarion and exclusive calls of Jesus in the gospel of John.[3] In response, Pilate simply quips, "What is truth?" (John 18:38).

In North American culture, we are constantly sold the lie that truth can be whatever we decide it is, which is to say there is no such thing as truth at all. Truth, we are told, is whatever *feels* true. But as the Christian hip-hop artist Lecrae says, "What if my truth says yours is a lie? Is it still true?"[4]

Jesus simply slaps this false notion to the ground.

The theme of truth is foundational in John's gospel. It creates stark contrast not just to Pilate's Roman context but also to the relativism of contemporary culture, as well as our socially and politically motivated power plays, where truth can be sacrificed on the altar of expediency and selfishness. Politicians and pundits may seem interested in *your* truth—so long as it advances *their* agenda, which is so often motivated by power and money.

Jesus' mission was to integrate truth into all of life—to live consistently and authentically as the perfect image bearer of God. Hearing and obeying Jesus is very different than simply affirming correct ideas about Jesus. Perhaps like Pilate, our questions about "what is truth?" allow us to easily obfuscate Jesus' claim of truth on our own lives.

What is the role of violence?

Every nation, civilization, and empire in human history has been built through violence, domination, and subjugation. This is because every government's power depends upon the ability to kill.[5]

Until Jesus.

Jesus' kingdom confronts the role of human violence and inverts it through sacrificial enemy love. Jesus defines true power as the willingness to lay one's life down for others, not dominating them through force or coercion. "Greater love has no one than this: to lay down one's life for one's friends" (John 15:13).

To be a nation or state, to have borders, to say this is ours and not yours, a government must have the power to exercise its will over others. Ultimately, the only way this can be done is through violence, or at least the threat of violence. Jesus says that is *not* the way of things in his upside-down kingdom. Jesus' kingdom is rooted in the ethic of love, and not coercion, which in its most potent form is violence and murder. In the trial before Pilate, this was the very thing the religious leaders were trying to exact on Jesus.

They wanted their will done, and to do so meant overcoming Jesus' will by killing him. Interestingly, the religious leaders did not have the power to kill Jesus, so they bogusly accused Jesus of attempting to overthrow Caesar. In a most fantastic twist, one that we still struggle to believe thousands of years after the fact, Jesus *willingly* succumbs to this. He does not retaliate, he does not resist through violence, and he does not repay evil with evil.

Like a beautiful aikido martial art move, Jesus completely reverses death's power by his submission to it—removing its sting by overcoming it through resurrection (1 Corinthians 15:54–56).

But standing there that night around the fire, the disciple Peter could not see that yet. All Peter could see was that he wanted a revolution, to be freed from the Roman occupation, and had put his trust and life into the hands of this rabbi from Nazareth. Now this revolutionary Messiah was being captured by the enemy—and he doesn't fight back? No wonder Peter pulled out his sword!

At this Jesus rebukes Peter and tells him that all who live by the sword will die in the same manner (Matthew 26:52). Jesus then proceeds to fix Peter's well-intended but ill-guided action by healing the guy's ear (Luke 22:51), confirming that his kingdom will not tolerate violence of any kind.

Just hours earlier, at the last supper, Peter had *sworn* that he was ready to die with Jesus (Mark 14:31; John 13:36–38). We have no reason to doubt Peter's sincerity. He was ready to die alongside his Messiah in battle against their oppressors and the blaspheming pagans set up against Yahweh, just as his countrymen had been in the Maccabean revolt two hundred years earlier.

But Jesus knew better.

He knew that Peter was ready to die with him in battle but was not ready to *willingly* lay down his life in the face of his enemies—yet. Peter runs for his life and follows Jesus at a distance after his arrest, perhaps looking for some opportunity to use force and violence to free his Rabbi. (It is safe to assume he still has his sword on him.) But once he hears the rooster crow, he recognizes his betrayal to his master's vision of a kingdom of peace. And he weeps bitterly (Matthew 26:75).

Peter's experience feels deeply relatable today. We want Jesus to be our Savior, but we also want to cling to the power of the world and be our own savior. We want to be saved from our sins and our enemies, but we don't want to lay down our lives and trust Jesus alone with the power over life and death. "My Father's will is that everyone who looks to the Son and believes in him shall have eternal life, and I will raise them up at the last day" (John 6:40). Instead, we want to defend our lives and those of our loved ones, just as Peter did, and utilize the tactics of the kingdoms of the world. In today's world, it is viewed as incredibly positive, if not downright required, to defend our loved ones with violence and death if necessary.

Jesus looks at us just as he did Peter and asks, "Will you really lay down your life for me?" (John 13:38).

Who decides what is right and wrong?

Jesus' confrontation with Pilate also involves a different understanding of righteousness. During Jesus' trial, Pilate becomes scared that Jesus truly is a king and attempts to make the people decide whether to kill or free him, even though Pilate found no basis for a charge against him. In this critical moment, the people shout that they want a known criminal, insurrectionist, and murderer to be set free instead of the innocent Jesus. In the shouts of the crowd we can hear how each of us clings to the power of the world and inverts righteousness with wickedness. We want the person who attempts to overthrow the oppressor with violence to be justified and set free, all while approving of the cowardly pacifist getting what they deserve. The kingdoms of the world often confuse, and even blatantly invert, right and wrong.

This distortion of what is right and righteous is at the very heart of the entire biblical drama. In Genesis 1–3, two image bearers of God, Adam and Eve, are created to enjoy union with God, one another, and creation itself. But they decide, with the help of a mysterious and deceptive creature, that they can gain autonomy from God and define good and evil for themselves—and so eat from the tree of the knowledge of good and evil in the garden of Eden.

This act produces a chain reaction of alienation and suspicion toward one another and God. The downward spiral of broken relationships, subjugation, slavery, and death continues all the way through the narrative to Jesus. Jesus himself hangs on a tree, unjustly murdered, exclaiming for God to forgive his killers because they don't know what they are doing, still wrongly defining good and evil for themselves (Luke 23:34).

In this story we see Jesus subvert Pilate's kingdom, one ruled with the iron fist of violence and domination, with nonviolent, self-sacrificing enemy love. After Jesus' arrest, his disciples hide in fear, but as Jesus stands exposed and stripped before the rulers of the world, he exposes and strips *them* of their power. "Jesus claimed absolute lordship but refused earthly throne, weapon, army, and image," writes scholar Gerald Sittser. "He demanded complete allegiance from his followers but sacrificed his life for them. He invited everyone to become citizens of his kingdom but had no territory over which he ruled."[6] If God looks like Jesus, then we see God offering his self-sacrificing love for the sake of his enemies. Even in the face of persecution, wrongdoing, and death, Jesus bids us to come and follow him, trusting in God for our final vindication and ultimate resurrection of life.

FOUR

A Cosmic War

The Apostles Follow Jesus into Nonviolent Battle

Jesus' first disciples, often referred to as the apostles (of which Paul says he was "one abnormally born" because he did not meet Jesus until after the resurrection), continued his nonviolent and subversive conflict with the violent powers and principalities of the world. Much of the apostles' understanding and practice of this nonviolent and peacemaking way is recorded within the pages of the New Testament. Jesus taught and lived out an ethic of nonviolence that demanded peacemaking, and it was nonnegotiable for his first disciples.

Though I am unable to address every relevant passage in the New Testament, the gospel authors consistently and thoroughly depict Jesus as nonviolent.[1] This consistent representation of the nonviolent Messiah continues throughout the New Testament in the book of Acts, the Epistles, and John's Apocalypse, called Revelation. To provide an overview of this consistency we will briefly look at the themes of nonviolent peacemaking and subversive resistance to empire in some of the writings of Paul, Peter, and John. If you are wondering about passages in the New Testament that seem to depict Jesus as violent, such as braiding whips and turning over tables (John 2), or Paul's acceptance of violence as God's wrath on evil (Romans 13), it is important to look at these situations in the context in which they happened in the Scriptures. We can err when we pull a passage out of its context or don't situate it within the larger witness of Scripture. I address these questions at greater length in the common questions at the end of the book.

Paul, the one abnormally born

Traditionally credited with authoring approximately half of the books of the New Testament (approximately a quarter by word count), Paul had plenty to say about his understanding of and obedience to Jesus, the Prince of Peace.[2] Luke depicts the story of Paul meeting Jesus clearly in the framework of violence. Luke introduces Saul while the gospel is spreading from Jerusalem, Judea, and Samaria to the ends of the earth (Acts 1:8). The first time we meet Saul, he approves of the killing of Stephen, a follower of Jesus (7:58), and is breathing murderous threats against the Lord's disciples as he actively persecutes them (9:1).[3]

Paul's encounter with Jesus on the road to Damascus leaves him blind for three days. His entire world is turned upside down by the Lord (9:17–19). Many years later, Paul described how his encounter with Jesus radically changed his understanding and practice of violence. "Even though I was once a blasphemer and persecutor and a violent man," he writes in 1 Timothy 1:13, "I was shown mercy because I acted in ignorance and unbelief."

Before meeting Jesus, Paul employed violence in what he thought was service to God. He followed the commandment to put to death anyone who blasphemes the name of the Lord (Leviticus 24:16), as he believed the Christians who said that Jesus was God were guilty of blaspheming. "I too was convinced that I ought to do all that was possible to oppose the name of Jesus of Nazareth," Paul says in the book of Acts. "That is just what I did in Jerusalem. On the authority of the chief priests I put many of the Lord's people in prison, and when they were put to death, I cast my vote against them. Many a time I went from one synagogue to another to have them punished, and I tried to force them to blaspheme. I was so obsessed with persecuting them that I even hunted them down in foreign cities" (Acts 26:9–11).

This life-changing encounter with the resurrected Jesus emboldened Paul with a new mission and a new understanding of God's kingdom, one that confronted evil nonviolently. Pauline scholar Jeremy Gabrielson says that nonviolence for Paul and the church communities he established was a constitutive part of the gospel of Jesus Christ. Paul's task of announcing the gospel to the nations involved calling and equipping assemblies of people whose common life was ordered and "characterized by peaceableness."[4]

As Paul spread the news of the risen Prince of Peace, he routinely used the familiar Roman legionnaire armor as a metaphor and imagery for spiritual warfare. Roman armor consisted of things such as swords, daggers, spears, shields, helmets, and breastplates. Paul routinely tells the Christians in Corinth that the weapons they are to fight with are *not* the weapons of the world (2 Corinthians 10:3–4). Paul repeats this message to the Christians in Ephesus when he reappropriates the Roman armory to the Christians and their battle, which is emphatically *not* against flesh and blood, but rather against the "spiritual forces of evil in the heavenly realms" (Ephesians 6:10–17).

As Christians we *are* engaged in battle. But ours is a *cosmic* battle.

We do not fight with the weapons of the world. But we possess weapons nonetheless. Our weapons are truth, perseverance, peace, righteousness, faith, prayer, and the Word of God.

Paul continues this same pattern of co-opting military metaphors when instructing his young protégé Timothy. "Join with me in suffering, like a good soldier of Christ Jesus," Paul writes. "No one serving as a soldier gets entangled in civilian affairs, but rather tries to please his commanding officer" (2 Timothy 2:3–4). This instruction comes in the context of remembering Jesus Christ—who has risen from the dead (v. 8), therefore we must be willing to die, enduring with him to the end (vv. 11–13).

Paul's military, combat, and warlike imagery gives us clarity into the role of nonviolent conflict and peacemaking for the Christian. It is not that we are free from conflict—far from it. We *are* in a battle and *are* to wage war—but we are to do it in a different way: a third way.[5] A way where evil is overcome by good and death is overcome by suffering love, a way that has been modeled by the firstborn from among the dead, Jesus himself (Colossians 1:18; Revelation 1:5).

Paul's commitment to nonviolence is not confined to ethics; it has political dimensions as well. Jesus' monikers "Son of God," "Lord," and "King of kings" have overt political overtones that would have been clear to the original audiences, meant to blatantly rival the authority of Caesar and all kings of the earth. The communities of Christians connected with Paul were called to participate in this new political order, one that was inaugurated by the Lord and starkly contrasted with every other world order.

The nonviolent life and message of Jesus, and subsequently Paul, challenged the status quo of the Roman political system by creating an alternative to it, a community of people that sought to overcome evil and enmity not by conquering or overpowering them, but by repaying evil with good (Romans 12:17–21).[6] It is in this context of Romans 12:17–21—not to repay evil with evil, not to take revenge, but rather to live at peace with everyone and overcome evil with good—that we come to the thirteenth chapter of Romans.

Romans 13:1–7, which begins with the line "Let everyone be subject to the governing authorities," has been used to justify all kinds of things contrary to the gospel of Jesus. It has been used by dictators to execute "justice" on whomever they deem an enemy of the state—as well as justifying the enslavement and abuse of minorities. Romans 13 is often looked to as an argument to support Christians being in the military and law enforcement because "the one in authority is *God's servant for your good* . . . For rulers do not bear the sword for no reason. They are *God's servants, agents of wrath to bring punishment on the wrongdoer*" (Romans 13:4, emphasis mine).

But is that really what Paul means, that Jesus followers are meant to be God's agents of wrath upon evil? A closer look reveals that Paul is saying the opposite: it is the empires of the world, not Christians, that are God's "agents of wrath." Paul says that the Christians in Rome are not to rebel against the authorities (Caesar or his legionnaires), precisely because it is God who rules sovereignly over the nations.[7]

Remember, this occurs in the context of Paul's instruction that Christians are to bless those who persecute them, not repay evil for evil, live at peace with everyone as far as it depends on them, and to not take revenge—because it is God's job alone to avenge. On the contrary, Christians should feed their enemies when they are hungry and not exercise wrath against them to bring them punishment (Romans 12:14–21). To look to Romans 13 as a justification for why Christians can use violence and kill as members of the military or law enforcement (in Paul's context the two were essentially the same entity of the Roman state) cuts completely against the grain of Romans 12. Paul presumes the existence of governments and authorities in chapter 13, and he is not advocating anarchy, rebellion, or revolt from Christians. Instead, he calls them to submit as citizens while also abstaining from systems that require violating the gospel of peace, especially when it pertains to killing and violence.[8]

For Paul, the theology of nonviolence is rooted in the resurrection of Jesus. The central fact of the resurrection makes nonviolence tenable. Paul states that without Jesus' resurrection from the dead, people would still be in their sins (1 Corinthians 15:17). And if there is no resurrection from the dead, then it would make logical sense that we should try to protect our physical lives at any cost, for death is the greatest thing to fear.

Resurrection is the foundation of all Christian nonviolence.

If the dead are not raised, then we cannot be freed from our fear of death (Hebrews 2:14–15), and we must cling to our lives at any cost, including employing violence. For "if the dead are not raised, 'Let us eat and drink, for tomorrow we die'" (1 Corinthians 15:32).

Peter, the reinstated rock

Peter is a hot-headed, short-tempered, passionate, and incredibly relatable follower of Jesus in the Scriptures. The one whom

Jesus said he would build his church upon (Matthew 16:18), the one who understood his brokenness and sinfulness before God (Luke 5:8), and who responded faithfully when Jesus asked his disciples who they believed him to be (Matthew 16:15–16). He is also the same disciple who emphatically said he was ready to die with Jesus in battle (John 13:37–38; Matthew 26:35), and then immediately proved it when he tried to kill those who arrested Jesus (John 18:10).

In 1 Peter, written many years after the resurrection of Jesus, Peter refers to Christians as "exiles" throughout the Roman provinces of Asia Minor (now northern and western Turkey). The exiles who received his letter were likely scattered believers from times of persecution in the Roman Empire. They lived in the world as temporary residents on the earth because their truest citizenship is in heaven (Hebrews 11:13; 1 Peter 1:17; 2:11). Theologian Stanley Hauerwas describes this attitude as being a resident alien.[9]

Peter's instruction about righteous living for these resident aliens in the world includes not repaying evil for evil or insult for insult, but rather repaying evil with blessing (1 Peter 3:9). This stands in stark contrast to many Christians today in the public arena who spew out venomous and poisonous threats, diatribes, and vengeance—often toward other Christians! No wonder nonbelievers find many Christians unbecoming and downright repulsive.

We are to live such good lives among the unbelieving world, Peter says, that even though we may be accused of doing wrong, our good deeds, righteous behavior, and nonretaliation will lead to them glorifying God on the day he visits us (1 Peter 2:12). Instead of rebellion and retaliation, in reverent fear we submit ourselves to human authorities, not only those that are good and considerate, but even those who are harsh (1 Peter 2:18)! This is contrary to the cultural narrative that teaches us to take nothing from no one and not allow ourselves to be subject to anything.

Jesus did not retaliate when he suffered; he made no threats—Peter says this is the example we are to follow. We do not need to retaliate, even when we suffer unjustly, because we can *fully* entrust ourselves to the one who judges justly (1 Peter 2:23). This means we can live completely free from the fear that violence tries to exploit, the fear of death. We are not to fear human beings, even those who can persecute and kill us.

Because of the resurrection, Jesus said we should not be afraid of those who can kill the body but cannot kill the soul (Matthew 10:28). Any righteous suffering, says 1 Peter 2:20, is a sign of God's blessing. So it follows that we should not fear what others can do to us, whether emperors, presidents, terrorists, criminals—even our own police. This is even more incredible coming from Peter, who some years earlier had misunderstood Jesus' kingdom and tried to establish it through the well-worn human patterns of violence and domination as he brandished his weapon in the face of threat.

John, the exiled revelator

Before I became a Christian, the first and only book of the Bible I had ever read all the way through was Revelation. I'm not really sure why. But there is no book of the Bible more weird, misunderstood, misquoted, miscalculated, misanalyzed, and misappropriated throughout history than John's Apocalypse.[10] And yes, John only had *one* revelation, even though the book is often mistakenly referred to in the plural as Revelation*s*.

The authorship of Revelation is debated by modern scholars. Tradition credits the apostle John, "the disciple whom Jesus loved," who wrote the fourth gospel and the letters 1, 2, and 3 John, with writing the book of Revelation. Revelation is a piece of apocalyptic literature written to seven churches in Asia Minor. Through John's prophetic pen, the risen Jesus addresses specific circumstances of these seven first-century churches as they face persecution, false teaching, and spiritual complacency and compromise.

Though Revelation has often been interpreted by mysterious number sets and signs thought to predict the end of the world, this was not John's intent in writing the letter. Instead, he offers a manifesto to stand against the powers of empire to a persecuted set of Christians in the Roman Empire of the first century. Biblical prophecy always addresses the contemporaries of the prophet's context as well as raises hopes that can transcend their immediate context and direct later readers to God's purpose for their future.[11] In this way Revelation has enduring relevance to lead every generation to follow the slain Lamb.

Chapters 4–5 of Revelation belong inseparably together and provide an important image for the entire book of Revelation—to hear and see. John gives the seven churches a framework to motivate them toward nonviolent resistance to empire.[12] In chapter 5, John is shown a vision where he "hears" that victory has been won and triumph over the enemies of evil and darkness has occurred through the Lion of the tribe of Judah, the Root of David (5:4–5). However, John "looks" and sees not a lion, but instead a slain Lamb who has the power to open the scrolls (5:6). The song John hears being sung by the living creatures and elders is *because* the Lamb was slain and "with [his] blood [he] purchased for God persons from every tribe and language and people and nation" (5:9). The word John chooses here for "slain" is *sphazô*, which means butchered, slaughtered, or murdered—instead of the word typically associated with ritual sacrifice, *thyô*. John never uses the typical word *thyô* for ritual sacrifice in the book of Revelation, but opts instead for *sphazô*, a word with murderous and criminal connotations, to talk about what has happened to Jesus. In other words, John is communicating that "Jesus is not a religious sacrifice. He is a political victim."[13]

The final book of the canon, Revelation is an apocalyptic vision of how victory over death and the power of evil is won through the blood of a slain Lamb named Jesus. John urges his audience to resist the temptation of vengeance while living under economic oppression and injustice, and instead invites Christians to peace and to overcome the dragon who leads the whole world astray, triumphing by the blood of the Lamb and the word of their testimony (Revelation 12:9–11). John's words prophetically echo with us today. As Revelation 18 attests, any society that absolutizes its own economic prosperity and military might at the expense of others comes under John's condemnation of Babylon (Revelation 18:9–20).[14]

FIVE

Swords into Plowshares

The Early Church Witness to the Sanctity of Life

Tradition holds that all the apostles, except for John (who was exiled to Patmos), were martyred for their faith. After the resurrection, there is no record of them trying to defend their lives, or those of their loved ones, in the face of threat or unjust death. This pattern held for the better part of three centuries as the early Jesus movement continued in these convictions around issues of violence and the sanctity of life.[1]

We have many writings from these early Christians from the first few centuries, often referred to as the church fathers, patristics, or ante-Nicene fathers (that is, church leaders writing before the Council of Nicaea in 325 CE).[2] While these writings are not considered part of the divinely inspired canon, I believe their proximity in time and culture to the teachings of Jesus and his earliest followers gives us a unique window into how Christians wrestled with and applied the Scriptures in the early generations after the ministry of Jesus. Though Christianity grew wildly in the first few centuries within the Roman Empire and beyond, even under times of great persecution and duress, it would be an error to overly romanticize and idealize the early church as if it embodied a kind of pure Christianity.[3] Even so, early Christian teachers unanimously insisted on the wrongness of killing, and their resoundingly consistent posture toward violence while living in an incredibly violent culture is instructive for us today.[4] They believed that all forms of killing were shortcuts, *signs of impatience* that were not appropriate for a follower of Jesus.[5]

Throughout church history, Jesus' life, ministry, death, and resurrection have provided a consistent pattern of nonviolent peacemaking that corresponds to a key element of Christian virtue. Christian peacemaking is not simply a utilitarian strategy to accomplish the outcome of peace (though it is proven to be highly effective), but rather a key trait of following Jesus.[6] The first few centuries of the church were known as "the age of persecution." Yet despite Christian persecution by Rome, this was also an age of pacifism—to the degree that no Christian author to our knowledge ever approved of Christian participation in battle.[7]

When we look at the witness of the early church, it is not enough to argue for Christian pacifism simply because that is what the early church taught and practiced—pacifism is also congruent with the life and teachings of Jesus himself. It is significant, however, that in a world where Christians were often the object of violence in the Roman Empire, they held fast to the nonviolent message of Jesus and were willing to give their lives before they would kill another image bearer of God.[8]

This nonviolent stance by Christians in the first three centuries was undergirded by their understanding that they were citizens of heaven first, while also remaining citizens of the world (see John 17:14–16; Philippians 3:20–21). As Donald Durnbaugh writes in *The Believers' Church*, a sense of "dualism between church and world . . . demanded a high ethic of Christians not expected in the secular realm."[9] For example, the *Epistle to Diognetus*, likely composed sometime in the late second century, says that Christians are "not distinguished from the rest of humanity by country, language, or custom."[10] While Christians followed the local customs in dress and food and other aspects of life, they also demonstrated the remarkable (and admittedly unusual) character of their own citizenship. In this view of reality, Christians participate in everything as citizens but also endure everything as foreigners and aliens at the same time. This perspective comes most sharply into focus when considering the issues involving the sanctity of life in military service, abortion, and healthcare practices.

Military service

Others have provided lengthy treatments of early Christians and military service, but even a sampling of early church writings is instructive.[11] Patristic writings from Justin Martyr in the early second century, not long after the book of Revelation was likely written, say that Christians renounced war as a part of their conversion to Christ, even if they were previously well conversant with war, murder, and everything evil. Converts to Christ, Justin contended, traded in their weapons of war for plowshares, and their spears for farm tools as Isaiah had foretold. "He will judge between the nations and will settle disputes for many peoples. They will beat their swords into plowshares and their spears into pruning hooks. Nation will not take up sword against nation, nor will they train for war anymore" (Isaiah 2:4; see also Micah 4:3).

Justin even proclaimed that Christians' stance on nonviolence was directly responsible for the growth of the church, arguing that the more Christians were persecuted and murdered, the more others became believers in increasing numbers.[12] Similarly, Irenaeus in 180 CE said that when Christians form their weapons into instruments used for peaceful purposes, they become so unaccustomed to fighting that when they are struck, they offer the other cheek also.[13]

No Christian author has written more on war and military service in the first four centuries than Tertullian. In the second century, he said that God prohibited "every sort of man-killing." He questioned how a Christian could go to war because he reasoned that even if soldiers came to John and received instruction on how to live (Luke 3:14), and a centurion came to faith in the Lord (Matthew 8:5–13), Jesus, by taking away Peter's sword in the garden, disarmed every soldier thereafter. Therefore Christians are "not allowed to wear any uniform that symbolizes a sinful act," such as the Roman military uniform.[14]

Origen, a brilliant and incredibly influential theologian from the late second century, said that Christians do not learn the art of war, since they have become children of peace through Jesus rather than following the traditions and customs of the kingdoms of the world.[15] Consistent with this perspective, he said that it is never right for disciples of Jesus to offer violence to someone, no matter how wicked they are, because Jesus did not allow the killing of any individual whatsoever.[16] In the early church, even self-defense was not an allowable situation for a disciple of Jesus to employ violence against someone.

Cyprian, of the early third century, said when Christians are persecuted for their faith, they do not attack their attackers, "since it is not lawful [in Christ] for the innocent even to kill the guilty."[17] He stated that though the world was filled with bloody horror and wet with mutual blood, even non-Christians recognize that it is a crime when an individual commits murder. However, he rebuked the notion that murder is called a virtue when it is committed wholesale on the grand scale of military conquest.[18]

Later in the third century, Lactantius said God forbids all kinds of killing, not only in war and the military but even with the mouth, by putting someone under a capital charge, such as in the case of a judge condemning a man to die via capital punishment. In the command to love your enemies, he said that "no exception at all should be made: killing a human being is always wrong because it is God's will for man to be a sacred creature."[19] The followers of Jesus in the early church had nonviolent reflexes when others treated them violently. They did not exact an eye for an eye but responded in silence and patience and even blessed those who cursed them.[20]

Nonviolence was an essential criterion when someone wanted to become a Christian in the early church as well. Church leaders would examine a person's vocation in order to be considered a candidate for baptism or to participate at the Lord's table. The *Apostolic Tradition*, dated by most scholars in the late 100s to early 200s, states that religious teachers must examine the professional behavior of all potential believers wanting to be baptized and require them to stop wearing the purple garments of the empire and give up wielding the sword.[21]

The scholar Eberhard Arnold continues with his own commentary on the *Apostolic Tradition* as he says the professions and trades of those who are going to be accepted into the community must be examined. The nature and type of each must be established. Professions such as a keeper of a brothel, sculptor of idols, charioteer, athlete, and gladiator must be given up or be rejected. A military constable must be forbidden to kill; neither may he swear; if he is not willing to follow these instructions, he must be rejected from the church. A proconsul or magistrate who wears the purple and governs by the sword shall give it up or be rejected. Anyone taking part in baptismal instruction or already baptized who wants to become a soldier shall be sent away, for he has despised God. Another version of the document adds that a soldier in the sovereign's army should not kill and if he is ordered to kill, he should refuse. If he stops, so be it; otherwise, he should be excluded from the church. These practices are also unacceptable: prostitute, sodomite, magician, and soothsayer. All these must be given up.[22]

The early Christian church would not allow people to convert if they were unwilling to give up professions that threatened human life.[23] In fact, the way of peace was a *prerequisite*, in keeping with repentance from sin, for people to enter the waters of baptism or participate in the Lord's Supper. Certainly, we have drifted from the moorings of our ancient brothers and sisters' anchors of faith on these issues.

Other issues around the sanctity of life

Early Christian stances of nonviolence were not only for military conscription, but all issues surrounding the life and death of human beings. Because of the fundamental conviction that all humans were created as image bearers of God, the early Christian view of the sanctity of life was consistent in matters of abortion, war, capital punishment, infanticide, and gladiatorial contests—even watching them.[24] For instance, the second-century document from Athenagoras, which claims to represent the commonly held Christian position of the day, says that abortion is murder and that the guilty must give account to God, and that the fetus is a living being, the object of God's care.[25]

It is greatly attested that abortion was frequently practiced by pagans in ancient Greece and Rome, and occasionally by Jews and Christians as well. Motives for performing an abortion were as varied then as they are today, including those related and unrelated to the mother's health. Though abortion was incredibly dangerous, the most common reason by far was to conceal illicit sexual activity, having both chemical and mechanical methods available in the ancient world.[26] Unfortunately, too many of us know the soul-damaging effects that ending an unborn life can cause parents. I personally came to deeply regret the decision I made with my teenage girlfriend—before I became a Christian—to voluntarily abort our baby because of the inconvenience that having a child presented us. This soul scar tissue perpetually remains.

It was a common cultural practice in the ancient world for infants who were unwanted or deformed to be discarded and left in the wilderness to die through exposure.[27] The early Christians earned a reputation for often taking these discarded children, adopting them, and raising them as their own. The early church spoke with univocal passion that both the killing of an unborn baby and the killing of a baby already born were the same thing: *murder*. In this regard Tertullian said,

> With us, murder is forbidden once for all. We are not permitted to destroy even the fetus in the womb, as long as blood is still being drawn to form a human being. To prevent the birth of a child is a quicker way to murder. It makes

> no difference whether one destroys a soul already born or interferes with its coming to birth.[28]

The early Christians believed so deeply in Jesus' resurrection from the dead that they did not shrink back from the things that would jeopardize their own lives, especially when it came to Jesus' command to love other humans (John 13:34–35).

In Rome, short-term hospitals were built for the empire's most precious economic commodity: soldiers and slaves—but there were no hospitals for everyday citizens, and no organized program for helping the sick. The early Christians had a reputation among the empire for caring for the sick, even when disease broke out. Eusebius of Caesarea records that Christians cared for the sick during a famine and plague in 312 CE. Some Christians were infected and died even while non-Christians abandoned their own family members to avoid contagion.[29]

Hippolytus of Rome in the third century, drawing on the teachings of Jesus in Matthew 25, said that whether a catechumen (someone who wants to become a Christian but who has not yet been baptized) regularly visited the sick was a measure of their readiness for baptism.[30] This foundation of loving others made in the image of God would lead to the first public hospitals by Christians in the fourth century, such as St. Basil's House of Healing.[31] This theology of the sanctity of life, that God alone is sovereign over life and death, must also intersect with our current practices of euthanasia and physician-assisted suicide (sometimes referred to as "death with dignity")—which are currently legal in eleven countries worldwide and ten states in the United States.

SIX

A Marriage of Two Kingdoms

A Seismic Shift

When I discuss Christian nonviolence with someone for the first time, especially in the context of Jesus and the early church, I can predict the inevitable question. It's usually something like, "So . . . how did we get here?" But behind that simple question is often a deeper confusion, maybe even a quiet grief: "How did we as the church get so far from the obvious teachings of Jesus? And why aren't those teachings obvious anymore?"

It's a fair question.

After all, when you read the Gospels with fresh eyes, Jesus' message is startlingly clear: love your enemies, bless those who curse you, turn the other cheek, put away the sword. And yet, somewhere between the early church and today, the radical ethic of nonviolence seems to not just have been softened but erased for many Christians.

The answer to how this happened is long and winding and far too complex to reduce to a soundbite—but there's a general consensus among historians and theologians about when the tide turned dramatically. There was a pivotal moment in the fourth century when something unprecedented occurred: Christianity, once a persecuted minority religion, suddenly found itself aligned with the emperor and imperial power.

This alliance would change everything.

Understanding that history, and the centuries that followed, is key to understanding not only how Christian nonviolence became obscured, but also how it might be *recovered*.

Unfortunately it's a story most haven't heard.

An unholy matrimony

When we look back at the early centuries of the Christian faith, what is most striking, at least to modern eyes, is the radical consistency with which the early church understood and applied the teachings of Jesus regarding nonviolence, enemy love, and the sacredness of life. For the first three centuries, followers of Jesus were unmistakably countercultural, choosing suffering and martyrdom over violence, even in the face of persecution. They believed that the way of Christ—turning the other cheek, loving enemies, blessing persecutors—was not just an ideal, but the very heart of what it meant to be Christian.

Then the church mutated.

This complex and nuanced mutation was punctuated by a seismic moment in church history: the conversion, or at least the political alignment, of the Roman emperor Constantine (306–337 CE) to Christianity. Whatever the authenticity of his personal faith, which remains a matter of scholarly debate, Constantine's embrace of Christianity dramatically altered the course of the church.[1] In 313, in the Edict of Milan, Constantine declared that Christians would be treated benevolently under

Roman rule.[2] Christianity, once outlawed and persecuted, now had a seat at the emperor's table.

This marked more than just a change in legal status for Christians; it initiated a sweeping transformation of Christian identity, theology, and public posture. The evolution is complex and often misunderstood, but it's clear a very different Christianity emerged. Prior to Constantine, no surviving Christian writing argued that a Christian could kill under any circumstance or serve in the military.[3] After Constantine, that consensus quickly dissolved.[4] As patristic scholar Louis J. Swift writes, "The reign of Constantine represents a watershed in the development of Christian attitudes concerning war and military service inasmuch as the question is no longer whether participation in war is justified, but what conditions should govern the right to declare war and what rules should be observed in waging it."[5]

The development of two cities

Augustine of Hippo (354–430) is one of the most towering figures in the entire history of Western Christian thought. Living just one generation after Constantine, Augustine found himself grappling with a new reality in church history: the Roman Empire was now considered a *Christian empire.*

In his monumental work *City of God*, Augustine wrestled with this dilemma. He drew upon classical philosophers such as Aristotle, along with Roman legal thought in Cicero, and sought to reconcile it with the teachings of Christ. Augustine didn't deny that Jesus taught nonviolence; rather, he believed that Jesus' radical teachings were given in a time when Christians lived under pagan rule. But now that Christians governed the empire, those teachings needed to be reinterpreted to account for the responsibilities of public leadership and civic duty.[6]

Augustine explained that "there is no such thing as a Christian empire, because the temporal and militant nature of empire is at odds with the eternal and peaceable nature of the heavenly kingdom."[7] In this context Augustine envisioned the Christian as living in "two cities": the city of God, where spiritual devotion and personal piety reigned, and the earthly city, where political responsibility might require force, and even death, in the pursuit of peace and justice. Thus, Augustine made room for a dualistic ethic: nonviolence in personal life, but potentially justifiable violence in public life.[8] Therefore, the Christian could, in theory, wield the sword for the good of the state—so long as it was done with right intent and under the proper conditions.[9]

This was a massive departure from the early church's view of the kingdom of God as wholly distinct from the kingdoms of the world, what I refer to as "two-kingdom" theology.[10] As Christians, we must navigate as citizens of the kingdom of God while living in a particular kingdom of the world, but we are to behave consistent with the ethics of Jesus. We belong to one kingdom, the kingdom of Jesus, and are to live consistently no matter what kingdom of the world we find ourselves in. James admonishes Christians who were fighting, quarrelling, and killing each other, calling them adulterous people because of their friendship with the world (James 4:1–6).

Augustine's work was in many ways a noble and thoughtful response to a rapidly changing environment, but it also opened the door to a redefinition of Christian discipleship that continues to shape the church to this day. Those in the United States, for instance, live under a form of government that allows its citizenry to shape its society through democratic republic means—at least in theory. This modern governmental model presents Christians with difficult questions about how to faithfully navigate fidelity to Jesus while working faithfully for love of one's neighbors and enemies, especially in public and civic spheres.

Later, in the thirteenth century, Thomas Aquinas further formalized Augustine's ideas into what is known as just war theory (or as some prefer, "just statecraft"), which establishes criteria for when war can be deemed just, and how it should be conducted.[11] These criteria are often divided into three categories: "the justice of war (*jus ad bellum*), justice during war (*jus in bello*), and justice after war (*jus post bellum*)."[12] Modern proponents of just war include the likes of C. S. Lewis and Reinhold Niebuhr. They base their thinking on the prior work of Ambrose of Milan, Augustine of Hippo, and Thomas Aquinas.[13] However, much of this work is rooted in the ideas of Roman statesman Cicero (106–43 BCE) when he articulated key themes defining just war in his *De officiis* (*On Moral Duties*).

Old Testament passages are often used to bolster this kind of position, as are New Testament passages such as John the Baptist's dealings with the Roman soldier (Luke 3:7–14), Jesus braiding whips and turning over tables in the temple (John 2:13–25), and Jesus proclaiming that the Roman centurion had faith greater than anyone else he had seen in Israel (Matthew 8:5–13). These interpretations often make an argument from silence, reasoning that if Jesus (or John the Baptist for that matter) wanted to teach pacifism, he would have told these soldiers to leave their professions as a part of their repentance into the kingdom of God. As I detail in the common questions at the end of the book, these passages were never intended to answer our questions about Christian violence, but rather were intended to answer different questions, primarily the understanding that God was now including every tribe, nation, and tongue through faith in Jesus Christ.

While ideas about the justice of war remain important and influential, the truth is that very few wars throughout history (if any) have met the criteria for just war. And yet, just war theory remains the default ethical framework for many even if they don't realize it. Just war is unconvincing for the follower of Jesus because it is primarily based upon human logic, philosophy, and ethics—over and above the life and teachings of Jesus as represented in the Holy Scriptures (along with the church of the first three centuries). It is true that some just war scholars, such as Eric Patterson, may find pacifist theological thinking "fantastical, idealistic approaches to the tough dilemmas of politics and society."[14] But I am persuaded to base my theological convictions on Jesus and to take him at his word.

Christians didn't envision using violence until they envisioned their nation being a Christian one. The implications of the Constantinian shift were not merely ethical, but theological and ecclesial as well—and they were not limited to topics of violence. For instance, scholar Dorothy A. Lee argues that the roles of women in ministry and leadership were varied and diverse in the early church and that any claim "to unanimity of practice are seen as anachronistic, reflecting a post-Constantinian setting."[15]

The church went from being a diverse and persecuted minority to being a privileged community in the empire as Constantine convened the Council of Nicaea in 325—partly to utilize Christianity's effectiveness in helping him unite the empire.[16] The church, no longer a persecuted minority, was now becoming an institution with political and military power.

Later, in the High Middle Ages (1000–1300), critics referred to this Constantine era not as a golden age of the church, but as the fall of the church—a time when the purity of Christ's teachings was compromised by political power and cultural assimilation. These radicals of the Middle Ages didn't invent the idea that Constantine's era marked a fundamental turning point; however, instead of seeing it as a victory for God and the church, they saw it as a defeat.[17]

From persecuted to persecutor

Through the fourth and fifth centuries, the fusion of church and empire accelerated. By the year 405, the Roman church/state enforced a single Christian orthodoxy against dissenters like the Donatists, a Christian sect whose resistance was met not just with theological argument but imperial military force.[18] By 436 all non-Christians were *excluded* from the Roman army, meaning all who fought must profess Christ. *Not* being a Christian now meant civil disadvantages, as public worship for any religion other than Christianity was outlawed.[19] At the beginning of the fourth century, pagan Romans were persecuting Christians with passion. At the end of the fourth century, *Christian* Romans were now persecuting non-Christians with equal fervor.[20]

In just under a century, as the Roman Empire became Christianized, the persecuted had now become the *persecutors.*

The symbiotic relationship between church and state, Christianity and culture that emerged in the Middle Ages came to be known as Christendom.[21] Interestingly it was this context that birthed the Christian monastic movement as the desert fathers and mothers began retreating from the compromised and worldly church of the fourth and fifth centuries.[22]

This marriage of Christianity with imperial force would reach a horrific crescendo in the Crusades starting in the eleventh century, when holy war was considered the highest calling of a Christian. Soldiers were encouraged to consider themselves the army of God and carry out the highest duty of a Christian: to kill others for the Christian religion.[23] Soldiers marched under banners of the cross throughout the known world, believing they were doing the will of God by conquering, enslaving, and oppressing other people. The sword that Jesus commanded Peter to put away, the sword that the early church had beat into plowshares, was now thrust through enemies of the empire—all in the name of Jesus.

The unholy matrimony of church and state didn't die with the Roman Empire, however. It would find new life in empires yet to come, such as the global ambitions of European colonial powers. These same ideologies fueled the expansion of the British Empire under the guise of Christian mission as it swept across India, Australia, Africa, and beyond—often with missionaries and soldiers walking side by side. Christian language and symbols were consistently used to justify domination, exploitation, and colonization as Britain became the largest empire the world has ever known at its height in the nineteenth and twentieth centuries—enslaving, taxing, and oppressing large swaths of the entire world.

This legacy continues to shape how Christians think about politics, war, justice, and the role of faith in public life, including in the United States, where Christian nationalism is on the rise. Today, we all live in a vastly different world than Constantine, Augustine, or Aquinas. Some of us are not the subjects of emperors, but rather citizens of a democratic republic. Yet we still wrestle with the same tensions: *How do we remain faithful to the nonviolent, enemy-loving ways of Jesus while participating in societies marred by sin and the fallen nature? How can we truly love our neighbors—and our enemies—at the same time?*[24]

These are not easy questions, but they are important ones.

In order to chart a way forward, following the Prince of Peace once more, it is vital to have some understanding of how we got here. If we are going to take the life and teachings of Jesus seriously, we must return to the Scriptures and take seriously the history of how his message has been adapted, reinterpreted, and distorted over the centuries. The Constantinian shift was not the death of the church or its witness, for even the gates of hell cannot prevail over the church—but it was a seismic turning point.

SEVEN

No Blood but Our Own

The Historic Peace Churches

As we continue our sketch of the past two thousand years of church history, we see violence, empire, and destruction proliferate as brutality and carnage wreak havoc during the Crusades and Spanish Inquisitions of the Middle Ages. Undoubtedly, remnants of Jesus' peacemaking and nonviolent ways have persisted among his followers through the ages, but broadly speaking, the dominant view of church-sanctioned violence continued unabated until the time of the Reformation in the 1500s. The Reformation was a major religious and political movement that challenged the authority of the Roman Catholic Church, leading to the establishment of various Protestant denominations. It was sparked by calls for reform regarding corruption and doctrinal disagreements.

Reformation of a reformation

Most well-known from this period is Martin Luther (1483–1546) and his famous Ninety-Five Theses, which were a protest of the sale of indulgences (among other things) in the Catholic Church.[1] He was a seminal figure in the Protestant Reformation, and his theology forms the basis for Lutheranism. Luther is widely regarded as a key influential figure in Western Christian history. Unlike Augustine, who treated Christian participation in state violence as a tragic necessity in a fallen world requiring constant moral restraint, Luther saw state violence as a God-instituted vocation through which Christians legitimately exercise the sword in service to neighbor within God's kingdom. In other words, Luther did not simply tolerate Christian involvement in the state's sword of violence but *theologically celebrated it* as part of God's providence. In fact, he stated that it was sin for a Christian to *not* use the sword in efforts to love their neighbor.[2]

Of all the things Luther did, perhaps one of his greatest and most enduring contributions was translating the Bible from Latin to German. Thanks to his work and the invention of the Gutenberg printing press around 1440, the Bible became widely available to be read by everyone, not just clergy. But even before Luther and the printing press, during the medieval period, there were forerunners to the Reformation, "proto-Protestants" if you will, who resisted imperial Christianity. Some of them were the Waldenses and the Unity of the Brethren.[3] The Waldenses, founded by Peter Waldo in the twelfth century, preached poverty and the authority of the Bible over the pope. These groups were persecuted for centuries during the Inquisitions as a cancer to the church because of their rejection of the pope and certain Catholic sacraments. Henry Charles Lea, a twentieth-century historian of the Inquisitions, says,

> There are few pages of history of humanity more touching, few records of self-sacrifice more inspiring, few examples

> more instructive of the height to which the soul can rise above the weaknesses of the flesh, than those which we may glean from the fragmentary documents of the Inquisition and the scanty references of the chroniclers to the abhorred heretics [such as the Waldenses and Brethren] so industriously tracked and so pitilessly despatched.[4]

The "believers church" movement began with the evangelical Anabaptists, commonly dated to the year 1525.[5] These Radical Reformers, as they were known, sometimes referred to as the Swiss Brethren for this branch's origins in Zurich, gave rise to what are today called the "historic peace churches," consisting of several Anabaptist traditions like the Mennonites, Hutterites, Amish, Bruderhof, Church of the Brethren, and others. Comparatively, these Christian traditions have historically been very small in number and have received intense persecution from other larger Christian traditions. The Anabaptist movement emerged in the wake of the Protestant Reformation and pressed for reform to move more quickly, and to break more sharply with established Catholic patterns than did mainstream Protestant reformers.[6]

There are several contours of the Radical Reformation that differed from the mainstream Protestant Reformation. A major one was their perspective on infant baptism and practice of adult baptism. The Radical Reformers, now able to read the Bible for themselves in their native tongue thanks to Luther, believed that the Christian rite of baptism was to be performed on those who were able to make a conscious decision to repent and follow Jesus as their Lord and Savior, and thus not to be practiced on infants. This earned the name Anabaptists (literally re-baptizers; the prefix ana- means "again") from other

Protestants, who persecuted them intensely, sometimes by drowning them—mockingly calling it the "third baptism."[7] The early Anabaptists were passionate about evangelism and spoke boldly to others about Jesus. In fact, they were so vocal that tongue screw torture devices were used to silence them by religious authorities.[8]

Let that sink in for a minute.

Christians had their tongues mutilated for talking about Jesus—by other *Christians*! It is often the case that those who follow Jesus are persecuted the most by those who think they are working for God (see, for example, Acts 4:1–12). These early Anabaptists were ready to suffer and die for their faith, as they understood the call to follow Jesus meant loving their enemies, even when their tongues were mutilated by them.

Anabaptist Dirk Willems is often named as an example of this readiness to suffer, even at the hands of one's enemies. Dirk Willems escaped from being imprisoned for his so-called heretical beliefs, and a guard fell through the ice in pursuit of him. Willems then turned around to save him from drowning. The act was famously rendered in an engraving by the Dutch artist Jan Luyken in 1685.[9] Dirk's rescue of his persecutor led to his recapture. He was burned alive in 1569 in what is now the Netherlands.[10]

The phrase "no blood but our own" eventually came to represent the conviction of those associated with these historic peace churches. While this may not be an official slogan, it effectively conveys the peace churches' ethos: a steadfast commitment to peace, a refusal to engage in violence, and a dedication to living out the teachings of Jesus in a world marred by conflict and violence, *even if it cost them, or their loved ones, their lives.*

The Anabaptists were also concerned about the purity and integrity of their church membership and wanted to be able to give an account of the faith of the people who were in them. In other words, church membership mattered. This was radical considering that for centuries the Catholic faith was largely propagated through bearing offspring, or the dominance of violence and threat of the sword, rather than through uncoerced personal confessions of faith. Anabaptists also believed that baptism was meaningless before a person had been taught, converted, and become a convinced believer for themselves.[11]

They believed that disciples were made, not born.

In 1527 a group of Anabaptists in Schleitheim, Switzerland, wrote the Schleitheim Confession. This confession came to represent the commonly held Anabaptist beliefs and principles. Written during a time of severe persecution, the confession consists of seven articles: baptism, the ban (excommunication of members), breaking of bread (communion), separation from the world (righteousness), pastors in the church (clergy), the sword (nonviolence), and not taking oaths (military conscription). The confession achieved widespread recognition a few months later, after the trial and execution of Anabaptist leader Michael Sattler by civil authorities in Rottenburg, Germany, who concluded that Anabaptism was immoral and treasonable.

Historian Edmund Pries notes that "the Anabaptist refusal to swear oaths was the most radical political act that could have been undertaken by anyone" because by doing so they made themselves ungovernable, taking away the state's primary tool of control—violence.[12] Oaths are promises that bind us to the state's way of organizing and ruling the world, through coercion and violence. As Mennonite pastor Melissa Floerer-Bixler comments, "After all, a pledge guarantees the possibility of perjury."[13] Because of this refusal to swear oaths, the Christian-state of the sixteenth century sensed threat and thus killed thousands of Anabaptists in the movement's first decade.

Yet, for those of us in America, in the public education system we are trained to pledge our allegiance to the state every single day (except perhaps on weekends).

People who sought reform of the Catholic Church, such as Martin Luther and Ulrich Zwingli (who also clashed with and persecuted the Anabaptists), worked to see a more authentic and less corrupt church in their day. God's Spirit also led the Scriptures to find a home in the hands and hearts of ordinary folks—which all led to incredible changes in Western Christianity. Perhaps similar to King Josiah finding the Book of the Law and tearing his robes (2 Kings 22), or the people's lament as Ezra and Nehemiah read the law for the first time in generations (Nehemiah 8), the radical life and teachings of Jesus, his apostles, and the early church around the issues of nonviolence found resurgence once again after being dormant for over a thousand years.

Treasures in jars of clay

As much as the historic peace churches have tried to reinvigorate the peaceable teachings of Christ, they have also sometimes struggled to embody their own ethics, as we all hold these treasures in feeble jars of clay (2 Corinthians 4:7). Though it was rare for Anabaptists to own slaves during the colonization of America, there were a few recorded instances where it happened, especially in the South, where social and economic pressures were greatest.

There were some abolitionist efforts in these groups, such as the Germantown Petition in 1688, when Mennonites and

Quakers drafted the first written protest against slavery in the English colonies. In the eighteenth century, Quaker pastor John Woolman fought for the abolition of slavery amongst Quakers, along with equitable treatment for Indigenous people.[14] Still, the historical record shows that while it was rare for Anabaptists to own slaves, not many actively opposed slavery or advocated for abolition. So what shifted between the generations of these faithful followers of Christ, once known for their fervent prayers while being burned at the stake?

Scholar Stuart Murray comments that separatist instincts endorsed by foundational documents like the Schleitheim Confession have been internalized by many Anabaptists today.

> At its worst, Anabaptist separatism has conveyed disregard for wider society and concern only for the maintenance and survival of their own families and church communities. The deep concern of many early Anabaptists for economic reform and social justice has not been passed on to many of their descendants. . . . The pressure of persecution gradually convinced Anabaptists that keeping quiet about the faith was the only way to survive, and most adopted this stance (some even signed agreements exchanging vows of silence for being left alone). They became known as "the quiet in the land" . . . but this nonverbal approach to bearing witness to Jesus Christ is seriously deficient in a post-Christendom culture that knows little of what Christians believe and lacks the tools to interpret the way we live.[15]

For some Anabaptists today there is a lack of outspokenness about Jesus—it is as though the silencing effect of the tongue screws are still in place centuries later.

The historic peace churches have a complex and rich history that has spanned continents, generations, and centuries. Some of these traditions, like the Amish for instance (sometimes referred to as Old Order communities), are popularly known for preserving a way of life from an era gone by with horse-and-buggy transportation, commitment to agrarian life and commerce, and refusal to adopt modern technologies. These groups may be considered cultural fossils by some, but many of them are committed Christians who have made rational choices to abate the cultural tides of modernity they believe can destroy the faith. There have been some instances of growth through evangelism in these communities, but the primary mode of expansion for these churches in the United States has been through ethnic and familial continuity—not through conventional outreach and evangelistic efforts as seen in the New Testament.[16]

However, we are *all* called to shine the light of Jesus' nonviolent, empire-resisting enemy love that has the power to transform households, neighborhoods, communities, nations, and indeed the world. It has been happening since the resurrection of Christ. But there are many, including in the historic peace churches, who need to be roused to action—not hiding the light of Jesus' peace and attempting to sequester it away safely in the hills of Pennsylvania, Ohio, or Idaho, far from the troubles of a broken and violent world. (In truth, communities removed from the larger fabric of society often face many of their own ethical and moral challenges.)

If we are honest, violence isn't something that is simply *out there*. It is something that is deeply inside each of us. A trumpet call is sounding for us to actively engage in a variety of

Spirit-led ways of peacemaking as we resist the urge to partner with the power that flows from empire, both inside and out.

Beautiful feet

In my own story, the Christian tradition where I became a Jesus follower didn't emphasize peace theology or nonviolence as a part of discipleship to Jesus. However, I'm eternally grateful for their emphasis on evangelism, seeking the lost, and taking the great commission of Jesus seriously—so a rebellious sinner like me would have an opportunity to respond to Jesus and the gospel of God's grace.

For those who consider themselves part of the historic peace traditions, please don't retreat to the caves of Qumran, or the hills of Pennsylvania, while letting the world go to hell in a handbasket! There are lots of people out there like me who *will* respond to the gospel—I invite you on Christ's behalf, be ministers of reconciliation in the world (2 Corinthians 5:18–21)! May Jesus help us all have feet that are fitted with the readiness that comes from the gospel of peace (Ephesians 6:15).

For truly, as Romans 10:15 attests, how *beautiful* are those feet.

The vision and heart of much of the Anabaptist tradition can serve as a well of living water for those residing in a cultural desert, especially in post-Christendom contexts like the United States. The kind of Christian spirituality that emphasizes submission to the lordship of Christ, obedience to the teachings of Scripture, the readiness to suffer for one's faith, open-handed generosity, a commitment to honesty and truthful speech—regardless of the consequences—and a refusal to kill—no matter the circumstances—offers a vision of Christ that will draw people to him who have been disgusted by the backbiting, hypocritical, and scandalous church that has often been co-opted by the state.

It is not Anabaptism as a Christian tradition for its own sake that I am concerned with, and I am certainly not saying that we all need to become Anabaptists—but I *am* saying that we should learn from all traditions as we become more faithful followers of Jesus.[17]

EIGHT

One Nation Under God

Christian Nationalism in the United States

In many ways I'm grateful I'm an American. There are many opportunities, freedoms, and comforts that are afforded to me because I am. Though I have a sense of gratitude for the country of which I am a citizen, I must also speak to the fact that it is not all good.

Many American Christians believe that America is God's nation. As scholar Lanta Davis puts it, this belief transforms Jesus Christ into "the American Warrior Jesus"—a mascot in red, white, and blue who "inspired the founding fathers, holds the Constitution, defends gun rights, and wields his cross as a weapon. Whether he's on posters, T-shirts, or bumper stickers, American Warrior Jesus is on America's side!"[1]

However, *no nation since the resurrection of Jesus can ever be God's nation.*

Through Jesus, God instituted a new covenant no longer defined by any national or ethnic identity (Matthew 28:18–20;

Romans 3–4). Unfortunately, many American Christians are often subtly (and sometimes not so subtly) assimilated toward Christian nationalism and secular culture in matters of militarism, violence, civic engagement, and self-preservation that veer from a biblical and historical vision of two-kingdom theology, Christian nonviolence, active peacemaking, and enemy-love. In many churches throughout the country there are Christians who insist that America is God's nation and that it was founded on Christian principles.

Of course this dynamic is not exclusive to America, as many countries and empires have claimed special favor with God. Since the beginning of Christendom in the fourth century, there has been a symbiotic relationship between church and state and Christianity and culture in the West. Though this is not exclusively an American issue, it is specifically an American one. As a Kenyan pastor said of those who consider themselves American Christians, "As a Christian you are my brother. As an American you want to be my master."[2]

These nationalistic ideologies and propaganda have seeped deeply into the psyche, identity, and politics of Christians throughout America. For instance, in Colorado Springs, considered to be the capital of American evangelicalism, the US Air Force Academy includes the most visited humanmade tourist attraction in all of Colorado (before its closure for renovations), the Cadet Chapel. The Cadet Chapel is a Christian chapel originally built in the 1960s (though now it is a house of worship for all faiths) that boasts a seventeen-spire exterior that resembles fighter jets, along with an interior cross hanging from the ceiling that is the shape of a giant sword.[3]

New Testament scholar and theologian Preston Sprinkle says that "a large portion of the American evangelical church has been seduced, whether knowingly or not, by nationalistic militarism. Yet our inspired Word of God aggressively critiques this very thing."[4] Germinating in the time of Constantine, sprouting through the Crusades and Inquisitions of the Middle Ages, and flowering in the British Empire of the nineteenth and twentieth centuries, Christian nationalism has flourished in the fertile soil of violence that has been watered with blood throughout church history. Today, Christian nationalism has become an invasive kudzu vine, choking out the truth of the gospel in America, and continues to thrive by the persistent myth that America is a Christian nation.

I believe there are many incredible things about America, and many ways that it brings about good. But Christian nationalism is more than a sense of patriotism or gratitude for one's nation, but the explicit amalgamation of church and state operating as one. It is a cultural framework—a collection of myths, traditions, symbols, narratives, and value systems—that idealizes and advocates a fusion of Christianity with civic life. In the United States, it includes assumptions that America has been and should always be distinctively Christian in its identity, values, laws, and policies.[5] In other words, Christian nationalism in America is the vision for a theocratic America with Christianity as the national faith that is tied to the state.[6] It is a worldview that becomes "a movement where one's God-given theological imagination is hijacked by political power."[7]

Scholars Christopher Hays and C. L. Crouch define it more colorfully, saying that Christian nationalism is "a bastard stepchild that does not require people to think about their neighbors as human beings, or to consider their neighbors' health and flourishing," most especially when those neighbors don't look like us.[8] This ideology is propagated by politicians, media, and a cultural narrative that uses a civil religion to justify empire. Georgetown political professor Paul Miller says that "much of American evangelicalism is acting more like a cultural tribe, an ethnoreligious sect advocating for its own power and protection, rather than a people from every tribe and nation advocating for universal principles of justice, flourishing, and the common good."[9]

From the nation's inception of European settlers and colonists there has been a belief that the budding nation was a chosen people of God. "Colonial preachers routinely compared New England to ancient Israel, suggesting that God had chosen the colonies for victory over Great Britain," writes scholar Richard Hughes. Even the founders embraced the myth that the new American nation represented God's chosen people, a kind of new Israel for these latter days. When Congress appointed Benjamin Franklin, Thomas Jefferson, and John Adams to design a seal for the United States, Franklin suggested a seal portraying Moses lifting his hand and the Red Sea dividing, with Pharaoh and his chariot being overwhelmed by the waters, and with the motto "Rebellion to tyrants is obedience to God." Jefferson made a similar suggestion: "a representation of the children of Israel, in the wilderness, led by a cloud by day, and a pillar of fire by night."[10]

From the very beginning, America was wrongly thought to be a chosen nation of God.

The cultural narrative of Christian nationalism was infused in ideas like Manifest Destiny, bringing the so-called light of European settlers in the East to the wild frontiers of the West. The allegorical 1872 painting *American Progress* by John Gast represents the Eurocentric modernization of the new West. In the painting, Gast personifies the United States as a floating blonde-haired white woman named "Columbia" who is leading civilization westward with American settlers. She is shown bringing light from east to west, stringing telegraph wire, holding a schoolbook, and ushering in different stages of economic and agricultural activity, along with evolving forms of transportation such as the steam engine. On the left, fearful and dismayed Native Americans, along with animals, flee from her—displaced from their homelands.[11]

The Doctrine of Discovery, a set of legal principles that provided justification for European colonial powers to claim sovereignty over Indigenous lands and peoples, was incorporated into the US legal system by the Supreme Court in the 1823 case *Johnson vs. McIntosh*. This "doctrine" persists to this day, even in my own public-school education, where I was taught that European settlers "discovered" the land and had been given divine right to it. This doctrine, along with a particular understanding of the Scriptures, fueled much of the conquest of the Americas by White Europeans in the name of Jesus.[12]

For example, Puritan preachers such as Cotton Mather portrayed White colonists as "the chosen people" who had a divine claim on American soil, and Indigenous peoples as disposable and despicable "Canaanites," similar to the conquest narratives in Deuteronomy 20:17.[13] Today, tragic stories continue to come to light about church-run residential schools where sexual and physical abuse, forced labor, and cultural genocide occurred toward Indigenous children in the United States and Canada. The American self-image as a "chosen people" has provided the rhetoric to mystify and justify domination, particularly over Blacks, Latine, Native Americans, and women.[14]

Many American Christians today still believe the narrative that America is God's country, and this belief obligates many of them to fight for the preservation and promotion of Christian culture and political influence.[15] Kristin Kobes Du Mez says that the belief that America is God's chosen nation—and must be defended as such—serves as a powerful predictor of intolerance toward immigrants, racial minorities, and non-Christians.[16]

Christian nationalism has pervaded American identity from the nation's origins, nourishing concepts like Manifest Destiny, which was not a specific or single law, but a powerful national ideology that blended religious fervor, white supremacy, and political idealism to justify the displacement of Indigenous peoples and the annexation of their territories. It continues to nourish practices today like the Oath of Enlistment required for all American military recruits:

> I, (NAME), do solemnly swear (or affirm) that I will support and *defend* the Constitution of the United States *against all enemies*, foreign and domestic; that I will *bear true faith* and *allegiance* to the same; and that I will *obey the orders* of the President of the United States *and the orders* of the officers appointed over me, according to regulations and the Uniform Code of Military Justice. So help me *God*.[17]

I respect many who serve in uniform, and I personally benefit from living in arguably the safest and most prosperous nation on earth, especially as a White man relatively free from danger and harm wherever I go.[18] However, you don't have to be a biblical scholar to see how this enlistment oath clearly contradicts the teachings of Jesus.

It is not hard to see how the past has shaped the nation's heritage as it blends God and country together into the vision of a single kingdom. Professor Mark Weldon Whitten writes that claiming America to be founded on Christian principles would "be at best, a monstrous oversimplification, and is in actuality a falsehood . . . to assert that the Founding Fathers were acting specifically as Christians in their efforts to found our nation, and that their intent was to create a 'Christian nation' through their efforts . . . is plainly a false-story myth of our national origins."[19] Yet this plainly-false-story-myth continues, nonetheless. I have had numerous pastoral sessions with members of my own congregation as they sat on my couch proclaiming that "America is God's chosen nation!"

Might makes right—right?

C. S. Lewis observed that it is the innocent who suffer in war, but the suffering of the peasant cannot be alleviated by banishing the knight.[20] This perspective underlines our cultural understandings of violence. But while this argument makes sense to our rational minds, Jesus upends our rationality, calling us toward faith and allegiance to God and his kingdom alone. We may find comfort in the belief that might makes right, and that peace only comes through war. But if we are honest, we recognize the complexity and ambiguity of determining who is truly "innocent" and who is not. Ultimately, peace through war does not point to the kingdom Jesus proclaimed.[21]

How are we to determine who is worthy of death, when Jesus told us to love our enemies? Can we love our enemy while at the same time killing them, even if for the sake of an innocent person? And how exactly do we determine who is innocent anyway? Who makes the cut for our assassination list?

Was Hitler worthy of assassination because he was responsible for killing some six million Jewish people and millions of others? What about the US pilots and crews who dropped atomic bombs that killed hundreds of thousands of civilians in Japan during World War II? What about the officers and president who ordered it, or the chaplains who blessed it?[22]

In another sphere, what about the doctor who has aborted hundreds of babies, or the hundreds of thousands of abortions that women choose in the United States *each year*? And what about court judges who sentence people to death in dozens of countries worldwide? Do we have a responsibility to kill these people because of their wickedness?[23] We must admit there is a great deal of complexity in these dilemmas. Often in our moral dilemmas of enacting justice via killing, it is those with higher socioeconomic means who end up deciding who is innocent and who is not (or at the very least affect the policies that do so), whereas those with lower socioeconomic status end up doing the dying.[24]

I recently attended a biblical scholarship conference where a person gave a speech about the changing cultural and intellectual perspectives around the world on the topic of euthanasia and legalized "assisted dying." Their basic point was that Americans need to be prepared for the theological shifts and philosophical justifications that are occurring in other places in the world that rationalize killing people at the (presumed) end of their lives.

The presenter did an excellent job and brought forward a very important topic about the nature of death and the sanctity of life. When they mentioned they were a retired US military officer, I wondered whether their value of sanctity at the end of life also applied to other times of life. After the presentation I asked them whether they believed Christians should ever kill under any circumstance. They said Christians have a responsibility to protect the innocent, even if it meant employing violence and killing, such as in war. "In that line of thinking," I asked, "wouldn't it be the responsibility of the Christian to kill the doctor who terminates innocent people at the end of their lives, such as in the practice of euthanasia you discussed?"

The presenter appeared to be stunned. I continued my line of questioning: "Wouldn't it also be the same for those who abort babies before their lives begin? Isn't this my responsibility to protect the innocent? As a Christian, wouldn't I have the moral responsibility to kill those doctors as well?"[25] I said that if someone takes the position that life is sacred and should not be terminated, in the womb or at the end of life, then they should be consistent in their approach throughout all of life and in all circumstances. Though this person was highly educated and a former officer in the US military, they said they had never thought of this and would need to consider it further. I was grateful for their humility and honesty, but it revealed to me just how deeply engrained the narrative of might makes right is.

Peace hidden from our eyes

I'm certain there have been groups and individual pacifists throughout church history that have been committed to Christian nonviolence, but the historic peace churches are most known for their official peace testimonies of Christian nonviolence and pacifism. Yet other Christian traditions have historically shared visions of peace as well, including the Assemblies of God, the Restoration Movement, Episcopalians, Presbyterians, Pentecostal groups, Catholics, and the Southern Baptists, who made a declaration in 1940 that "war is contrary to the mind and Spirit of Christ."[26]

The tradition where I was introduced to Christ shared roots with the Restoration Movement (or Stone-Campbell

Movement) of the Second Great Awakening in the nineteenth century. This movement was deeply established in Christian nonviolence and pacifism at its beginnings, even though most of its membership today is unaware of this. During the American Civil War, the Disciples of Christ (a branch of the Restoration Movement) is estimated to have had the largest proportion of pacifists of any southern denomination except for the historic peace churches.[27] David Lipscomb, a key leader in the movement, along with the *Gospel Advocate*, the largest publication in the Churches of Christ, strongly advocated pacifism among the churches of the South.[28] By the time the United States entered into World War I, the fellowship of the Churches of Christ was the largest peace church in the country.[29]

This characteristic of nonviolence among Restoration churches suffered decline in the twentieth century. In 1918, as a direct result of intense antipacifist sentiments that swept the United States during WWI, Cordell Christian College in Oklahoma, a Church of Christ university, closed under government surveillance and community pressure. O. E. Enfield, a leading Oklahoma preacher and socialist, was imprisoned at Leavenworth for his antiwar sentiments.[30] The largest Pentecostal branch, the Assemblies of God, also abandoned pacifism around the time of WWII, in 1937.[31]

The attack on Pearl Harbor further shattered confidence in pacifism, and many began to believe US involvement in the war was a justifiable means to stop the evils of Nazism (and other Axis powers like Japan).[32] The US government played a vital role in these changes—the *Gospel Advocate* was threatened with losing its mailing privileges unless it stopped promoting pacifism among its members. Under pressure, the publication changed course and reversed its position on nonviolence.

Though there were some pacifist influences after the war, pacifism was largely relegated to a matter of personal opinion in many churches.[33] By the 1980s most in the Churches of Christ had become pro-military, conservative Republicans.[34]

In one generation, nonviolence as a foundational tenet of discipleship all but disappeared across large swaths of American Christianity.

The story is the same across much of the evangelical South in the second half of the twentieth century. The implicit theology of Christian nationalism looms in the background, if not blatantly in the foreground, but often has not been challenged or examined in any meaningful way.

As a college pastor at a prominent state university in Alabama, for instance, I once confronted a student who was tailgating outside the football stadium with a sign above him that read "Life Priorities: 1. God, 2. Country, 3. 'University Name' Football." He was standing on top of a pull-behind trailer with multiple kegs, pouring beer funnels to the students below. As I approached, he asked me if I wanted a pour. Declining it, I told him that if he believed what the sign said he needed to stop pouring—or needed to take the sign down. He got down from the trailer.

In my city, and in many others like it, you will find decals on the windows of cars and trucks that read, "I stand for the flag and kneel for the cross," a clear symbol of how faith and nationalism are conflated. This conflation is everywhere. For instance, one popular Christian band borrowed their name from the British war cry of English soldiers, "For king and country," saying it has become their mission to lay down their lives for their King [Jesus] and their country.[35]

Du Mez puts it bluntly: "What sort of Jesus are [evangelicals] imagining? Is their savior a conquering warrior, a man's man who takes no prisoners and wages holy war? Or is he a sacrificial lamb who offers himself up for the restoration of all things?"[36] How we answer this question reveals who we understand Jesus to be, as well as what it looks like for us to follow him personally and collectively.

Unfortunately, we don't have to look very hard to see what it looks like for many evangelicals in America to follow Jesus. Rioters breached the US Capitol in Washington, DC, on January 6, 2021, which came to be known as the Capitol Attack. This group of largely evangelical rioters was in protest of Donald Trump losing the presidential election in 2020. As of 2026, more than one thousand five hundred people have been charged with federal crimes. Several people died during the event, and four police officers who were on the scene later committed suicide.[37] Many of the rioters were Christian nationalists, and several people carried signs with Christian messages. A video showed one man in a fur hat and horns leading others in a prayer inside the Senate chamber.[38]

I don't mention this to berate a particular politician or political party, for God knows that politicians of all stripes use Christian rhetoric to justify state-sanctioned violence and all kinds of evil. But the Capitol Attack reveals a deeper motivating worldview and understanding of Jesus for so many in America—a belief that America should be a Christian nation led by Jesus, the conquering warrior who takes no prisoners.

This blending of Jesus and America in the Capitol Attack is perhaps somewhat ironic because after a meeting in 2012 when pastors laid hands on Trump in prayer, he reportedly said, "Can you believe people believe that [BS]?" Writer Peter Wehner notes, "It's hard to imagine a person who has less affinity for authentic Christianity—for the teachings of Jesus, from the

Sermon on the Mount to the Parable of the Good Samaritan—than Donald Trump."[39] Yet evangelical Christians, including some members of the historic peace churches, have consistently given him great support

Mennonite pastor Melissa Florer-Bixler suggests that modern Anabaptists who supported Trump in the 2024 election did so out of a survivalist instinct primarily for economic reasons, not the teachings of Jesus. She writes, "The history of ethnic Mennonites is a history of receiving the spoils of whiteness even as these communities fenced themselves off from active participation in the violence required to realize their (white) economic and social gain—from colonization of the Americas to relying on the police to protect their private property."[40]

Whatever your political affinity, the Capitol Attack, along with other political trends, reveals a complex social and religious reality in America. Of course, this is not unique to America, but this intricate fabric is woven with the threads of Christian nationalism and a particular way of understanding Jesus.

NINE

God and Guns

America and the Myth of Redemptive Violence

Any claims that a soldier can kill someone in war and at the same time love the enemies they are killing are not credible—whether made in the era of Augustine or today. As minister Craig M. Watts has written, "Love reflective of the cross endures suffering rather than inflicting it and accepts death rather than causing it."[1]

Protecting life is often viewed as the highest moral good; therefore killing in order to protect people has become the norm and implicit theology of most American Christians today—what theologian Walter Wink calls the myth of redemptive violence. From a Christian worldview, our biological lives are a precious gift from God, and intentionally terminating life is evil—but in view of the resurrection of Christ, our biological lives this side of resurrection are *not* our highest good. Therefore, death is *not* the greatest evil.[2]

The myth of redemptive violence enshrines the belief that violence saves, that war brings peace, that might makes right. President Barak Obama, for instance, said after the assassination of Osama Bin Laden, "[Bin Laden's] demise should be welcomed by all who believe in *peace* and *human dignity*."[3] Wink argues that redemptive violence is one of the oldest continuously repeated stories in the world, and that it is the foundational myth of the modern world and the dominant religion in our society today.[4] It is "the story of the victory of order over chaos by means of violence."[5]

As I write this it is the anniversary of 9/11. President Donald Trump released an official proclamation that September 11 henceforth be referred to as Patriot Day, because "my administration is committed to upholding a foreign policy of peace through strength, and we proclaim without reservation that any enemy who seeks to strike our shores, endanger our citizens, and threaten our way of life will be met with devastation and crushing defeat by the fiercest, most lethal, and most formidable military on the face of the Earth. . . . We vow that any enemy who spills American blood will face the full wrath of American justice."[6] Admittedly, at one time in my life this kind of statement would have gotten me pumped, but this is a radical departure from Jesus, who commanded his followers to love their enemies.

Jesus said to love our enemies and pray for those who persecute us; we say that any enemy who threatens us will be blown to smithereens. Paul said to leave wrath and vengeance to God alone; we say that anyone who spills our blood will face the full wrath of American justice. This ideology is summed up well in the classic spoof spy thriller *Get Smart* when the villain is blown off a cliff by a trick-loaded cigarette. Agent 99 watches in horror and says to his colleague, "You know, Max, sometimes I think we're no better than they are, the way we murder and kill and destroy people." To which the other agent retorts, "Why, 99, you know we have to murder and kill and destroy in order to preserve everything that's good in the world."[7]

From *Mission Impossible*, *Top Gun*, or *Teenage Mutant Ninja Turtles*, the myth of redemptive violence has saturated the minds and hearts of most American Christians today, despite the New Testament's clear testimony of Jesus' life and teachings being defined by nonviolent enemy love. This myth is what socializes and indoctrinates virtually all children, especially young boys, and is ultimately driven by profit margins—not the interests of maturing citizens who have high values, ethical standards, honesty, compassion, or noble character.[8]

This myth is also what undergirds the common belief that only a good guy with a gun can stop a bad guy with a gun. But Preston Sprinkle is right: "If the only way to stop a bad guy with a gun is a good guy with a gun, then the only guy I want to see packing is *Jesus*. He's the only good guy I trust. *And he's packing, alright.* But his weapon is a cross not a gun, and he calls his followers to pick up our own."[9] The myth of redemptive violence says that violence is the only way to ultimately stem violence, even though there is a mountain of data and research that shows this simply isn't true.[10]

Most soldiers, no matter what country they serve, tend to start off thinking they are the good guys. However, this perception often erodes for soldiers who experience combat. If you have an honest conversation with a soldier from any country who has been in combat, you will tend to find that the boundary lines—between good and evil, right and wrong, the good guys and the bad guys—are not so easily distinguished. "A true war story is never moral," writes Tim O'Brien in his short stories exploring the Vietnam War.

> [A war story] does not instruct, nor encourage virtue, nor suggest models of proper human behavior, nor restrain men from doing the things men have always done. If a [war] story seems moral, do not believe it. If at the end of a war story, you feel uplifted, or if you feel that some small bit of rectitude has been salvaged from the larger waste, then you have been made the victim of a very old and terrible lie, there is no rectitude whatsoever. There is no virtue. As a first rule of thumb, therefore, you can tell a true war story by its absolute and uncompromising allegiance to obscenity and evil.[11]

Even the lauded special forces of the military—the tip of the spear—are not as glorious as portrayed on-screen. Just the other night my wife had a pastoral meeting with a young woman she had recently met. The woman sobbed as she talked about being separated from her husband and on the brink of divorce. Her husband was in the military and for the past couple of years had been away training with special operations of an elite tactical arm of the military. She lamented how she numbed the pain of the first year through substance abuse in her efforts to cope. More recently it had gotten so bad that she feared for her own safety when he was around. She confessed how much he had changed as he was being trained to disassociate and disconnect from pain—even from reality itself. She remarked that he essentially undergoes torture in his training and preparation for combat. He now suffers from severe PTSD—and has yet to be deployed.

The reality of what it takes to create elite human killing machines is rarely depicted on-screen. What is paraded in pop culture are the hero narratives that perpetuate the mythic narrative of God and guns in America. But humans are not meant to be made into killing machines. It fractures the mind and the soul.

We fight with worldly weapons

Americans comprise approximately five percent of the world's population but own approximately half the world's guns! With nearly four hundred million guns in the United States, there are more guns than people—a truly unique phenomenon on the world stage. More Americans have died from guns in the last fifty years than all the wars throughout American history.[12] Yet there is a strong God-and-guns culture among many who claim to follow Christ.

Consider the Florida gun manufacturer that designed an assault rifle called the Crusader, engraved with the words from Psalm 144:1, "Praise be to the Lord my Rock, who trains my hands for war, my fingers for battle." The safety switch on the rifle has three settings: Peace, War, and God Wills It. But this is nothing new. The fusion of God and guns goes back to the earliest gun marketers in America, who were called missionaries. The early Colt revolver was called the Peacemaker, an obvious ode to Jesus' teaching about being a child of God.[13]

Now that the scales have fallen from my eyes, I can't unsee it.

The implicit and explicit messaging of God and guns is *everywhere*. Living in the South, my wife's friend was given a beautiful new leather-bound Bible, along with a shiny new pistol resting on top of it—tied together as a birthday present from her husband. She proudly posted pictures on her socials.

In a restaurant in Atlanta recently I saw a young Black man wearing a shirt that word-played the familiar phrase "In God We Trust" by replacing God with the name of a popular handgun manufacturer: "In Glock We Trust." The layers of meaning of him wearing the shirt are complex—pain, oppression, protection, irony, resistance. A Black pastor once told me she wanted her husband to buy her a handgun to keep in her car because she was afraid of driving in rural Georgia by herself during pastoral visits. After our conversation she confessed she had never considered how that practice might intersect with Jesus' teachings on nonviolence.

In the mountains where I live, a White man down the street said he believes in the way of Samson, that "most problems can be solved with the jawbone of a donkey." This reference to Samson's vengeance on the Philistines when he killed a thousand men with a jawbone in Judges 15 was a clear metaphor that he believes violence is the way to solve problems—apparently not realizing that Samson is depicted as the lowest point in the cycle of judges and brought under strong critique by the biblical author.[14]

This is what American Warrior Jesus looks like.

Surveys among Americans show that people want guns to protect themselves and that self-defense is the primary reason given for gun ownership in the United States. Women frequently cite protection as their *only* reason for owning a gun. Interestingly, Christians in the United States are more likely to own guns than non-Christians.[15] In one survey of practicing Christians, nearly three in five agreed that it would be acceptable to defend themselves with violence if necessary, which closely mirrors the attitude of the general population.[16] Since 1979, more Americans have been killed by guns than all service members who have died on the battlefields of *all* US wars since 1775.[17] Guns now cause more deaths in the United States than automobile accidents.[18]

God-and-guns culture runs deep. Recently I was at a restaurant and saw a man wearing a shirt that said "Faith, Family, Freedom," emblazoned with a cross and American flag. These Christian nationalist icons and messages are everywhere, especially in the South where I live. The Second Amendment of the US Constitution is undergirded with language that bearing arms for the security of a free state is a right of the people which cannot be infringed. Notably, when this constitutional amendment was written, it was a right only for white people. Today this right is often interpreted as a "God-given right."[19]

The political battle over gun legislation and the Second Amendment is vigorously fought by many, including the National Rifle Association (of which I was a member in my youth). But gun legislation has been quite selective throughout history. In 1857, the Supreme Court in *Dred Scott v. Sandford* ruled that African Americans—enslaved or otherwise—had "no rights which the white man was bound to respect." This included the right to own guns, for fear that enslaved Black people would revolt. I can't imagine why! The Second Amendment, ultimately written by White men for White men, has historically been interpreted to keep guns out of the hands of people of color, in particular Black, Brown, and Native American people.[20]

Many people I know own guns simply out of fear, fear of someone who is *other*.

This fear is exploited by huge interest groups, extremely well-funded corporations, and the sociopolitical consciousness of the nation, not to mention church pulpits. We are told that loving your neighbor—whether they be your family member or a nation halfway around the world—means protecting them from harm even if it comes down to killing as a last resort (though if we are honest, it is usually the *first* resort). If we remove the emotional elements from this line of thinking, we see that the logic translates basically as follows: I should love my enemies, feed them, clothe them, and pray for them—except if they should threaten my life, my loved ones, or a someone I think is innocent halfway around the world. If me and mine are threatened, then I can kill.

If this were correct theology, then it would be the Christian's *moral obligation* to protect the innocent—even with violence and killing if necessary. This means that every Christian *should* be armed to the teeth (as they often are in my context). An extreme example—but still a logical outcome—of this mindset is when the pastor of Unification Sanctuary in Pennsylvania had his congregation bring their AR-15s to church so they could pray over them and bless them. This occurred just days after a school shooting in Florida.[21] More common examples are when I see congregants, even elders and pastors, carrying firearms into church services while they worship Jesus—American Warrior Jesus.

Can you imagine Paul telling the Christians in Corinth that we don't wage war as the world does, nor do we use the weapons the world uses (2 Corinthians 10:3–4), except for our AR-15s when we want to protect ourselves? This way of thinking is sadly common among many Christians. But when Jesus' church acts according to its calling to be his holy bride, it understands itself to exist in a condition of *permanent tension* with the ways of the world—because the world pursues its goals through methods that are at odds with the kingdom of the cross.[22]

We enjoy violence

The opening story of the book of Genesis chronicles the creation narrative and God's crowning achievement of creation: humanity (Genesis 1–2). We don't get three pages into the story before we realize the major conflict in the rest of the biblical plot: Humans have rebelled against their Creator and against their designation of corulers and cocreators. Instead they seek autonomy to define right and wrong for themselves, taking from the fruit of the tree of the knowledge of good and evil (Genesis 3). The very next thing that happens? One of their offspring, Cain, murders his brother Abel because "sin was crouching at his door" (Genesis 4).

Humans killing humans is a central theme in the biblical narrative, and one that is arrested and revolutionized by Jesus. In fact, the Bible boldly contrasts all other human mythologies by showing that the mark of Cain and his violence in the story of Genesis 4 is the defining sign of civilization itself. But the cross of Christ is the sign of salvation, overcoming violence through the nonviolence of love and forgiveness.[23]

If we look closer at America's obsession with guns, we will find an even deeper reality. We find ourselves in a conundrum around Jesus' nonviolence and enemy love because, if we are honest, the simple truth is that we idolize and enjoy violence. In what I find to be a shockingly transparent admission, theologian Stanley Hauerwas notes that we say we want peace, but in actuality we love conflict and war.[24] And Old Testament professor Christopher Hays points out that American Christians are far more profoundly violent than anything found in the Old Testament, because as Americans we are *entertained* by violence. We choose to watch it on television and in movies, to listen to it in song, and even to enact it ourselves in incredibly realistic and immersive video games—all for our entertainment. It's true that the "prevalence of violence in our culture *makes us increasingly desensitized to it.*"[25]

Dave Grossman, a retired lieutenant colonel from the US Army, with coauthor Gloria DeGaetano, say that children in our culture have gotten accustomed to killing primarily because of the steady diet of violent television, movies, and video games that desensitize them to violence. Lt. Col. Grossman says this is very similar to the military's sophisticated conditioning techniques used to overcome soldiers' natural aversion to killing, and that "media violence primes children to see killing as acceptable."[26] School shootings are but one manifestation of such violence. As of 2024, nearly two-thirds of the shooters at school mass shootings in the United States were under the age of seventeen.[27]

Amid our cultural obsession with and enjoyment of violence (to which I am certainly not exempt), one of the most powerful tropes in contemporary pop culture is one that renews and recharges an ethos of sacrifice: *socially approved revenge.*[28] Socially approved revenge is repaying evil with violence until our sense of justice is satisfied, and everyone cheers.

I personally love *Star Wars*, *The Lord of the Rings*, *Braveheart*, *The Count of Monte Cristo*, and many other great stories of revenge. And my children love them too. When my two young boys started watching cartoons, it didn't take long before I recognized this trope of socially approved revenge *everywhere*.

We tend to approve of revenge socially because violence and revenge ultimately reside inside us. We want justice. Our desire for justice is not wrong—in fact, it is part of our nature that bears the image of God. But our implementations of justice usually manifest as violence and revenge, which is the first and greatest connection between God-and-guns culture in America. Ever since we ate from the tree of the knowledge of good and evil and decided to take that moral decision-making into our own hands, we have been violent—and banished from Eden.

TEN

Let God Sort 'Em Out

A Southern Congregation's (Reluctant) Journey into Nonviolence and Hope for a New World

The congregation where I pastor is a smaller church made up of diverse people in both age and ethnicity, comprised of families, singles, students, children, and retirees ranging from infancy to those in their eighties. In 2020 I taught a series on the book of Revelation and began speaking out publicly against Christian nationalism for the first time in my pastoral career. A couple of years later, after a catalytic event in the church, the leadership team decided to devote an entire summer to the topic of Christian nonviolence after we were confronted with the question of how we understood nonviolence and the gospel of Jesus, particularly as it pertained to vocations such as the military and law enforcement. After much discussion, prayer, and consideration, we concluded that it was something that should be taken seriously and decided that I should start teaching publicly on the subject.

We knew that most, if not all, of the congregation had very little prior exposure to this way of understanding Jesus. Prior to the summer of public teaching on nonviolence, we guided our small group leaders through a yearlong discussion of Christian nonviolence and read a short book on the subject together. That summer I preached sermons and the congregation engaged in small group discussions to process together. We studied, wrestled, questioned, and wondered together. As I taught, I also tried to listen to the hearts and minds of people trying to live out their faith in a world of violence.

We devoted four sermons and four communion experiences to engaging in Christian nonviolence. In the series I discussed a war of two kingdoms, where we looked at the nature of Jesus' kingdom in conflict with the kingdoms of the world, especially around matters of violence and power in John 18. We discussed Christian nationalism and the blending of two kingdoms, looking at nonviolence throughout church history, particularly the Constantinian shift. Then we talked about the role our fear of death plays into our understanding of using violence to defend ourselves, and concluded by engaging the differences between peacemaking and passivity and discussing the active, nonpassive nature of Jesus' nonviolence.

We also made room for small group discussions in between each of the sermons to allow congregants to share what they were honestly thinking and feeling with one another. They discussed what they had learned from the previous sermon, what was most challenging or difficult and why, and how the teaching affected them personally. They also talked about what changes they might make because of the teachings, along with what impact they could have on society at large.

Because I was also drawing on this process as part of my doctoral research, we offered anonymous surveys before and after the series that asked people to reflect on questions like what their exposure to Christian nonviolence theology was prior to the series, to rate their fear of death, and to consider whether they agreed that America was God's chosen nation. I also conducted personal interviews with several members who participated in the surveys and small group discussions.[1]

At first, I was a bit nervous. How would this be received? What would people think of me? How would my colleagues react? *Would I keep my job!?*

My own process of coming to share my convictions about Christian nonviolence with our church leadership, and then the broader church, took some time. After first talking with my immediate family, I then approached my leadership team, where I communicated that my convictions around nonviolence, and their implications, might mean that I was no longer the best fit to be the pastor of the church. I told them I had counted that cost and would respect whatever decision they might make—but that I must be faithful to what Jesus has called me to. But above all, we needed to take time as a leadership team to discuss the issue. It was the first time any of them had ever heard about nonviolence explicitly.

Most people I was around had never been explicitly exposed to Christian nonviolence theology. I mean, let's face it, in my twenty years of following Jesus, I had never heard it preached, much less preached it *personally*! Most had grown up with an image of Jesus that was inseparably linked with nationalism, military strength, and personal protection—just like me. When I began discussing the idea of preaching about it, I talked with a good friend of mine who was a pastor. He said he had never heard of Christian nonviolence and asked me if there were any books on the subject. Shocked, I said indeed there are![2]

As a church we were going to be challenging some core assumptions—not just about theology, but about identity, culture, and patriotism.

But amid these challenges, something beautiful happened.

We can't unsee it

Take Bob, for example.[3] Bob had been part of our congregation for years. A retired police officer, he had followed Jesus with deep devotion most of his adult life, so much so that he taped index cards with Scriptures written on them inside of his patrol car. One of those verses? You guessed it: "Love your enemies" from the Sermon on the Mount. He had read those words hundreds, maybe a thousand times—but as our series on nonviolence progressed, he confessed, "It's like I'm reading these verses for the first time. What else in the Bible have I unknowingly done this with?"

Bob wasn't alone.

Most of the folks who participated in the anonymous surveys rated themselves highly when asked how seriously they attempted to follow Jesus' teachings in daily life. I'm convinced this was a critical part of the journey toward our community embracing a new vision of Jesus and living in his kingdom. In fact, not one person rated themselves below a three out of five. I guess this is why Paul urges us to think of ourselves with sober judgment (Romans 12:3)!

No doubt these folks were earnest. Gina described her daily walk with Jesus like this: "From waking to going to bed at night, I try to be the most loving person I can possibly be." Kevin said, "It's about Jesus being Lord over every aspect of my life." And Mary offered a more contemplative response: "I want to walk with Jesus all day, and to hear his voice and stay present with his Spirit, even in mundane activities. I want to obey what he says in my thoughts, attitudes, relationships, and decisions—and when I mess up, repent and walk in the light through transparency with others."

God, guns, and fear

When people genuinely love Jesus yet have a foundational misunderstanding of who he is, and who he calls us to be, there are often several factors at play. Therefore, I approached the sermon series by illuminating some of these factors that can be difficult to perceive. I talked about the history of our current assumptions and understandings of God and the acceptability of violence, noted how our faith tends not to liberate us from our fear of death as it should, and discussed the importance of pacifism not being passive.

Fear, it turns out, is often the root that drives our God-and-guns culture. Fear of death, chaos, and not being in control. But the entire Bible consistently echoes the refrain *do not be afraid*.[4] When I spoke with Rhonda about our church's sermon series, she shared that she was most affected by reflecting on why people are violent in the first place: "Basically, the fear of death," she said. "I had never really contemplated that before." Rhonda also shared that she and her sister, whom she lived with, were seriously considering getting rid of their gun because of their growing Christian convictions around nonviolence. Another congregant, Terrance, candidly admitted to me in a private conversation that before the series he simply believed we should "kill 'em all and let God sort 'em out." That popular phrase, based on a line from the Crusades of the thirteenth century, is a deformed depiction of the God that Jesus said we would behold when we look at him (John 14:9).[5]

When I asked people about their fear of dying, most said they weren't afraid of death itself but rather of pain and suffering, or the impact their death would have on loved ones, especially young children. I also asked survey participants about Christian nationalism and whether they believed America is God's chosen nation. Only one person strongly agreed. The others scored their belief as two or lower out of five, with the vast majority rating themselves the lowest possible score of one.

In my experience in Southern evangelical churches, this is pretty rare.

The anti–Christian-nationalist view among many people in our church was likely due to our specific geopolitical landscape and because the church had been steeped in several years of teaching that challenged this narrative. In the surveys and interviews, folks revealed their aversion to Christian nationalism by colorful remarks such as, "Pffft," "Brainwashing poppycock," "That's crazy talk," "That's just silly," "That's nuts," "That seems ridiculous," and "Dang, I didn't know Jesus lived in America."

"Because of cultural indoctrination, I used to believe this, but I do so no longer," one participant wrote. "As I have grown as a disciple, my patriotic indoctrination has come more into conflict with what I read in Scripture. Learning more about Jesus and nonviolence, I feel a freedom to discard my earlier unwavering devotion to America as an instrument of God and embrace my full loyalty and devotion to Jesus' teaching of nonviolence."

Another person told me they had a negative visceral reaction to the teachings about anti–Christian-nationalism—they felt like they had a pit in their stomach. Though they couldn't necessarily explain why, they had a knee-jerk and almost subconscious reaction to sermons that spoke against Americans being God's chosen people. "You brought in good questions about how much jingoism have I accepted in terms of my walk with God regarding America," they shared. "Is it America first? Is it God first, America second? How has commercialism, the media, and historians colored my viewpoint towards actions that the country and politicians make? How am I handling that? Which prism am I seeing these things through?"

As you may imagine, the topic of gun ownership sparked deep reflection for many here in the South. When asked whether owning a gun is a God-given right, most said no, but some were unsure, or possibly conflicted. The surveys did not parse out nuances about the many possible reasons why a Christian might own a gun, or the circumstances in which one might use it—for instance, hunting—yet it revealed deep enmeshment stemming from the Second Amendment.

For many, however, there was a strong separation between a God-given right and a human-given right. Billy put it bluntly, "I don't believe any rights of this world are given by God. I believe that the right to bear arms is protected by the Second Amendment for United States citizens and has nothing to do with the Christian faith." Others admitted they'd never thought about the question before.

For some, the question about gun ownership brought up issues of self-defense. One church member shared how his dad was "a gun guy." His dad, a small business owner, had carried a pistol for most of his life. "As a jeweler, he was aware of people who might try to rob him, and he was in the Army, had training, but is generally a peaceable guy. Now he owns a lot of guns and ammo. He tried to persuade me to get a gun permit when we moved to Florida, but I declined. America is not the new Israel. The church's weapons are prayer, persuasion, and enemy love."

One of the most significant shifts in the church came when we talked about killing via state-sanctioned war. The sermon series occurred in 2023 during the beginning of US involvement in the Russia-Ukraine war, so naturally some struggled with the application of Jesus' nonviolence in this context. Jenny's remarks were insightful:

> The US is the weapons vault of the world. A large part of our federal budget is allocated to maintaining a standing military. The "military-industrial complex" which Eisenhower warned us about is very much alive and well. . . . US churches have been oddly silent regarding this, often pledging loyalty to whatever US policy sends our armies abroad. The church has not influenced the nation with a blessed are the peacemakers ethos. The nation has co-opted the church into blessing the troops.

Jing, originally from Malaysia, reflected on her sister's experience during two robberies at her home in Malaysia as we considered how Christians might respond if they are threatened with violence. "I have never been in that kind of challenging situation, where I would find out if I would respond peacefully," Jing shared. "That would be a question I hope to answer if God puts me in that situation—but I don't know." She said that seriously investigating Jesus' life and ministry had helped her consider nonviolent options should something like that arise. It was valuable to see her international and cross-cultural perspective interplay with the nonviolent teachings of Jesus, illuminating that our cultural biases shape our understanding of him.

Issues around self-defense proved to be another fault line where shift occurred. In the beginning, just under half of the survey participants believed it was not justified for a Christian to own weapons for self-defense—by the end of the series that number had jumped to 72 percent! Matthew said, "I used to think self-defense was justifiable, but that was just cultural acceptance. I'd never wrestled with it with the Bible open." Theologian Preston Sprinkle notes that the logic justifying killing someone as a Christian ultimately requires the belief that "Jesus is still in the tomb, prayer doesn't work, a deistic god stands off in the distance, and the deception of power has clouded your Christian thinking. But my world, the real world, has a crucified Lamb, an empty tomb, and direct access to the heavenly throne which is more effective than 10 tons of C-4."[6]

Blessed are the peacemakers

Not all ambiguity was cleared up by the end of the series for everyone, of course. Understandably, some continue the process of wrestling with the Lord and the Scriptures, which is all any of us can do. After the series our congregation has continued to find ways to implement our understanding of Jesus as the Prince of Peace. But I will never forget the story of how one man's life was transformed.

Before the series, Shen and I had a three-hour conversation where he asked me about the killer at the door scenario. This is the scenario that we all tend to think of—what would I do if there was a murderer who broke into my house and threatened my family? (This scenario receives longer treatment in the ethical questions at the back of the book.) During the discussion,

Shen began to soften to the idea of Jesus' call to nonviolence and wrestle with the implications of the several New Testament passages we discussed. As it would turn out, after the sermon series Shen had an encounter in his home not so unlike our discussion.

Shen and his family live next to a golf course. One day, a man was walking in Shen's yard while a few of the man's friends stood in the driveway. After several minutes of this, the man marched to Shen's front door and began to beat on it incessantly. At the time, Shen was at home with his three young children. As he recounted the story, he told me how nervous he was, not knowing what the man was going to do and having flashbacks to his childhood when he was bullied and beaten because he was a racial minority. Bullied by people who looked like the white man now standing agitated at his front door. In that moment he said he remembered our conversations and began to wonder what Jesus would have him do to peaceably love this man—rather than meet him with anger, fear, and aggression.

Shen opened the door and kindly greeted him.

The man, who was noticeably angry, said he was missing his phone from the golf course across the street, and the GPS tracker showed it was inside the house. After Shen denied that he knew anything about the phone, the man became even more belligerent when he spotted a black phone on the coffee table inside, insisting it was his. Instead of arguing or continuing to deny it, Shen simply invited the man inside to check for himself while his children sat on the couch in shock.

The man was stunned—hesitant to come inside because of what weapons Shen might have inside. After his hesitation he decided to come in and check the phone on the table. After he realized that it was not his phone, Shen showed him hospitality by asking him if he would like to sit down and offering him something to drink. Bewildered, the man said, "No thanks." He and his friends quickly departed.

When Shen walked outside, he saw his neighbor, who quickly came over. Apparently, he had been watching the event from his yard with his sidearm at the ready in case "anything went down." Shen told me that because of his intentional wrestling with the Scriptures to understand Jesus as nonviolent, the Spirit helped him engage this situation differently than he would have otherwise. Shen also now noticed the stark contrast of his neighbor's response.

This was not unlike my retired police officer friend Bob. Bob was also radically transformed through our church's wrestling process. After the summer sermon series, he said that the words "Love your enemies" landed differently for him. So much so he did something incredible—he got rid of all his firearms: nine handguns, ten rifles and shotguns, and ten thousand rounds of ammunition!

Blessed are the peacemakers, for they will be called children of God.

Most in our congregation grew up in the thick of the Southern American Christian experience. In this context there is often a deep longing and sincere desire to follow the risen Messiah. Many in the South genuinely love Jesus. But often they have only heard of a particular version of Jesus that is skewed from the Scriptures. Given the chance to communally explore Jesus' call to nonviolence, many will respond with open hearts and minds.

This shows that people's beliefs and actions *can* change.

Even when these beliefs are implicit or deeply embedded through cultural history, fear, jingoism, families of origin, political narratives, and theological traditions. But our church's experience doesn't have to be unique. Others, perhaps *many* others, will be ready to walk this path—one where they can be gently led, given space, resources, and a new vision of Jesus. Much of our task is simply identifying the water we swim in. We are all shaped by our contexts—and if we are not aware of them, they can make us feel beholden. They can twist our understanding of God, Jesus, and the gospel. In a country where Christian nationalist ideologies are deeply engrained and often assumed, we need the courage to name these distortions and turn to the Lord in repentance, trust, and faith. If not, we risk continuing to baptize our culture's obsession with violence in the name of Christ.

But it doesn't have to be that way.

I share our church's example not to imply it is the only way, but to show that careful and communal wrestling can help shape hearts and minds, even when we are deeply saturated and shaped by our cultural contexts. Peace is not just an unrealistic idealism; it is *central* to the way of Jesus. I'm convinced that more Christians, across various traditions, are beginning to rediscover this. Many Catholics, for instance, the tradition where just war is historically rooted, are returning to gospel nonviolence, while many others are reclaiming commitments to peace as well.[7]

Christians *can* be formed more into the likeness of Jesus and become peacemakers, even while living amid empire and the reality of Christian nationalism. This shift can create ripple effects that reduce gun violence, transform conflict, and heal families and communities. This can happen even though we live in a time when gun deaths are all too common, especially among children.[8]

The church's conviction and posture of peace must restore a distinguishing mark of the Jesus movement to a gun-dying world. We have an opportunity to stand up with compassion and clarity, shining forth like stars in the darkness (Philippians 2:15). May this starlike brilliance result in relationships, households, neighborhoods, workplaces, and communities experiencing the leaven of peace and love—even while living amid conflict, hatred, discord, jealousy, and war.

ELEVEN

Exilic Outposts

Subversive Resistance and Uncivil Worship

A form of Christianity has long served as a civil religion in America.

But Christianity is no civil religion.

A civil religion is not a formal religion, but a system of meaning that provides a sense of collective identity and purpose to bind a nation together. America has long used Christianity for such purposes. However, Jesus' kingdom transcends all civilizations, nations, and kingdoms of the world—and calls those from every nation to join him (Matthew 28:18–20; Revelation 7:9). In a dominating context of civil religion in America, we must resist empire. In every context that utilizes a civil religion in the name of Christ, we must practice what scholar Michael Gorman calls *uncivil worship*—the rejection of civil religion. The book of Revelation provides a manifesto for how we might do so as it presents "a sustained stripping of the sacred from secular power—military, political, economic."[1]

This kind of uncivil worship has occurred throughout church history, beginning with those who rejected the power of empire in the first few centuries. It continued through small pockets of Christianity, then the historic peace churches of the Radical Reformation. Some suggest that one of the earliest recorded instances of uncivil worship and nonviolent action happened in Egypt approximately three thousand five hundred years ago when Hebrew midwives, because of their fear of God, refused to obey Pharaoh's command to execute Hebrew baby boys (Exodus 1:15–2:10).[2]

Following the king of a kingdom that is *not* of this world while living in a nation *of* this world requires great discernment and wisdom. In the postmodern and increasingly post-Christian Western world, we are witnessing the death of Christendom and the church's loss of cultural power.

I, among others, think this is likely a good thing.

But how do we navigate this landscape? A landscape dominated by vitriol and online defamation. A social context that doesn't create space for honest and decent dialogue or know how to disagree with civility, but instead casts everything in the shadow of us versus them.

Do we dig in our heels, shout a battle cry, and wage culture wars against an increasingly pagan landscape? One where morality is driven by feelings and preference to the point where "all moral disagreement is rationally interminable"?[3] Or do we take the Benedictine monastic option, like the Amish, and withdraw further from society to create isolated communities of resistance while the world continues to slip down a slope to nowhere?

I cannot spell out precisely how followers of Jesus should navigate peaceful resistance and uncivil worship in every political, governmental, and societal context.[4] I trust the Holy Spirit to lead us in that regard. However, "Jesus is no draftsman of political blueprints," wrote German pastor and theologian Dietrich Bonhoeffer just prior to WWII. "The cross is the only power in the world which proves that suffering love can avenge and vanquish evil."[5] This is especially the case for those of us who live in a democratic republic and can participate in shaping our society—at least in theory.

If you vote, you must know that you are *always* voting for a sinner and ultimately voting for the lesser of evils. While we are called to pursue the good of others to the best of our ability—which can include, and perhaps at times necessitate, voting—ultimately, putting our hope in legislative policies to create the kingdom of God on earth is a fallacy. And one that political pundits will often exploit.

A Christian nation-state was never in view for Jesus. As disciples of Jesus our goal isn't to create a Christian state or to maintain or resurrect some form of Christendom. Rather, peace-building and enemy love are multidimensional in the kingdom of God, consisting of gradual and fallible human processes that involve moral dilemmas and challenges along the way.[6]

A third way

So how do we live in this land of Mars that is saturated with violence and vengeance? To actively engage in uncivil worship, we must return to what Christians of the second century started calling the "third way," or more recently, what church history scholar Stephen O. Presley calls "cultural sanctification."[7] This third way seeks to navigate between the two extremes of the binary fight-or-flight responses as the gospel "simultaneously indigenizes itself to the local culture and reminds the church that she is a pilgrim in this world and must be out of step with the culture where it conflicts with the call of following Jesus."[8] In other words, we must live out our faith while living in a culture that is hostile toward authentic Christianity. While we are embedded within our culture, we must seek its sanctification (both personal and corporate) by pursuing virtue.[9]

One of the historic Christian virtues of the third way is *nonviolence.*

However, Jesus and the New Testament authors did not have in mind simple ideological pacifism alone. "The problem with 'ideological pacifism,'" writes theologian and ethicist Myles Werntz, "is that it tempts humanity to deny its creaturehood, by retreating from the contingencies of life, assuming a moral response as knowable apart from the ongoing movement of God in history, assuming an appropriate response before God has called for it in the midst of life."[10] In other words, Jesus does not call us to retreat in seclusion to escape the kingdoms of the world because of our convictions of nonviolence. Nor are we able to know for certain based on principle alone how we might respond in any given situation. I for one have considerable doubts that I might respond nonviolently in some circumstances. Instead we are to faithfully, albeit fallibly at times, struggle to live out Jesus' kingdom vision patiently while rubbing up against—and often coming into conflict with—the kingdoms of the world.

One of the most pragmatic questions about all this is whether nonviolent action and peaceful resistance *work* in the real world.

Are we just to be nonviolent lambs for the slaughter? Can anything ultimately be made right without the use of might? There are powerful testimonies throughout history as well as modern examples of the efficacy of nonviolent resistance. The nonviolent civil rights movement in the United States led by Martin Luther King Jr. is of course a famous one, along with Gandhi's nonviolent resistance to achieve Indian independence from Britian. In fact, there is a growing body of research that shows nonviolent action can be *more effective* than violent action to bring about lasting peace. But as theologian Ronald Sider has perceptively pointed out, *the problem is that so few of us have tried it!* He notes that "pacifists have long claimed that they have an alternative to war. But that claim remains empty unless they are willing to risk death, as soldiers do, to stop injustice and bring peace."[11]

There are a myriad of imaginative applications for active Christ-centered peacemaking in our world that can transform conflict in our homes, congregations, neighborhoods, cities, and nations. And it doesn't need to begin with some grand-scale social justice cause. Simply look at your own heart, your own home, your own workplace. Is there some way you are using violence, coercion, or manipulation to get what you want?

The lowest-hanging fruit of Christian enemy love is simply not desiring to kill our enemies, both individually and nationally. But there are other imaginative pathways to peacemaking that can shape us as well. For instance, as a father I have had to reconsider the relational dynamics with my children and the ways I express power and authority over them, including not domineering over them by using my physical and intellectual power. As parents, my wife and I also engage in conversations with our children about the narratives of violence and revenge that we see all around us while trying to limit their exposure to violence in media—an uphill climb to be sure. I am forced to continually consider how to "teach peace to children who play war."[12]

Perhaps this kind of active nonviolence seems insignificant when compared to the horrors we see around us, but even our small efforts can lead us toward communal flourishing that can radically shape everything from racial reconciliation to environmentalism, criminal justice, abortion, and immigration issues.[13] The Christian activist Shane Claiborne and others in the RAWtools organization have found creative and powerful paths toward peace by offering conflict resolution training and blacksmithing events that turn unwanted guns into garden tools—literally beating our modern-day swords into plowshares.[14]

If Christians are to prioritize and value the nonviolent enemy love of Jesus, we must have the moral acuity to perceive the dominating patterns of social power, and have the gumption to live in such a way that we resist violence, not just in matters of war, but in our daily lives.[15] Martin Luther King Jr. said, "Nonviolence is not sterile passivity, but a powerful moral force which makes for social transformation."[16] It is also important to remember that political activism is not the only means to achieve lasting peace—many Christian brothers and sisters throughout history have had no political options available to them, yet they were beautiful peacemakers.

Resisting (white) male-dominated violence

We must be mindful in our peacemaking efforts because they are not always just, nor consistent.[17] For instance, some of us, including peace theologians and practitioners, may reject violence in war and genocide while accepting (or being less inclined to recognize) the violence of sexual abuse and gender-based discrimination. Christians and churches can reject violence at the state and national level but fail to address violence on an interpersonal level, in the pulpit, and in the home with spouses, children, and animals when we "kick the dog."

Patriarchy as a misogynistic enterprise has long been an acceptable form of violence, especially toward women and children. This has historically gone unaddressed even in discourse among Christian ethicists.[18] We need what theologians Myles Werntz and David Cramer call *Christian antiviolence*: active resistance to sexual and gender-based forms of violence, whether interpersonal or societal. "The problem with peace theology in the context of war," they note, "is not just that it forgets to pay attention to interpersonal violence in addition to state violence, but that it gets war and state violence wrong by not recognizing that each are already sexually violent."[19]

Violence is a gender-discriminant issue.

When I talk with people about Christian nonviolence, it is hardly ever women who object. It is almost always *men*. Men own guns at triple the rate of women in the United States (64 percent compared to 22 percent) and commit 89 percent of all murder-suicides and 85 percent of all homicides. Of the ninety-six mass shootings in America between 1982 and 2018, all but two were committed by men or boys, and most were white men.[20] (The trend continues for mass shootings after 2018 as well.) In his book on the RAWtools movement, Shane Claiborne recalls hearing a woman theologian say it makes sense that God came as a man in Jesus, so we could see what a redeemed male looks like—and to assure us that men *can* be loving and gracious and caring like God![21]

Scholar Lauren Winner has said that you might drive past a church called Church of the Good Shepherd, but not likely the Church of the Mother Hen.[22] But both are accurate biblical images of God. Especially for men, it can be easier to think of

God as a warrior who sanctifies violence and war, but often it's because we've allowed our masculinity to change how we understand God—rather than allowing God to change how we understand our masculinity.[23]

Womanist theologian Monica A. Coleman challenges a patriarchal, White, and abstract notion of pacifism and urges us to resist violence not by simply rejecting aggression, but by nurturing life and connection amid spaces that are meant to destroy them. Nonviolence, therefore, is not a passive endurance, but an act of survival and community-making in the face of systemic and interpersonal violence. "Survival itself is a theological act," Coleman writes. "To continue to live, to love, and to create in the midst of violence and oppression is to participate in God's work of making a way out of no way."[24]

Outposts of peace and beacons of hope

In America, Bibles and devotionals specifically published and tailored for vocations that require killing other humans abound. Though they undoubtedly sell lots of copies, this understanding of the kingdom of God harkens back to the fourth century through an unholy matrimony between the kingdom of Jesus and the kingdoms of the world. This marriage of two kingdoms has not only endured but often thrived.

After the seismic shift with Constantine in the fourth century, the blending of church and empire led to a radical drift away from understanding Jesus primarily as the Prince of Peace. Instead of compelling the love of enemies, Christendom often used Jesus to justify atrocities like the Crusades, Inquisitions, and the destruction of Indigenous peoples across the world, including later empires of the world such as the United States of America. The church justified itself as it destroyed other

Christians, murdering those who would defy the papal state for the sake of pursuits like science, compassion, and conviction—and enslaved and eradicated entire cultures and civilizations for its own economic domination. This mirrors the thief that Jesus described who came to steal, kill, and destroy (John 10:10). But Jesus promises that he has overcome the world and that the gates of hell cannot overcome the church he began (John 16:33; Matthew 16:18).

The church has been arguing about the role of violence for Christians for the better part of five hundred years. Anything the church argues about for that long is not stupid—nor is it simple.

No matter where or when you read this book, the subject of violence and peacemaking will always be relevant. It's what digital creators call evergreen content. No matter what time in human history, no matter what nation, culture, or civilization you find yourself in, this subject will always be relevant.

That is because war is always happening somewhere on the planet. *At all times.*

If we are going to take Jesus seriously and understand God most clearly through him, we must renounce violence, resist the colonization of empire, and practice peacemaking and enemy love in every area of life and at every stratification of society. In the violent world of Mars, we are a type of exile, and our key identifier as citizens of another kingdom is nonviolence.

Living as outposts of peace is no small task, but there are many others like me out there, and many other congregations like ours, where people are simply waiting for the Christian message to challenge them to a heroism worthy of their lives—a heroism of nonviolent action![25] My prayer is that more Christians will be able to perceive the cultural influences that shape us in ways contrary to the kingdom of Jesus. It is the task of each generation of Jesus followers to figure out what it means, both in theory and in practice, to follow him in their context.

We will not know how to solve all the problems of violence in the world this side of new creation, but we know that all enduring solutions *start with Jesus*. The New Testament reveals Jesus as the fulfillment of Isaiah's prophecies, the Prince of Peace, who taught his followers to be peacemakers and renounce violence. Jesus himself, as the exact representation of God (Hebrews 1:3—literally the character and image of God[26]) was nonviolent and loved his enemies, even to the point of giving up his life in the face of unjust and horrific violence—entrusting himself to the one who judges justly (1 Peter 2:23). Yet he did this while subverting violence with nonviolence and destroying death through resurrection. The apostles and earliest Christian communities unanimously followed in Jesus' footsteps for centuries, even unto martyrdom—all while the message of faith in the Prince of Peace spread throughout the empire.

But let's be honest; the road to peace is tough, and we must prepare for action—for this "war against war is going to be no holiday excursion or camping party."[27]

We live as foreigners and aliens in this world—outposts of peace amid ubiquitous violence. We do this filled with hope while waiting for a new world. But who hopes for what they already have (Romans 8:24)? We wait patiently in hope, at times in agony and groaning that words cannot express, and we do not abandon this world to destruction, but actively live as peacemakers in our homes, our workplaces, our communities, and our nations as the Spirit creatively leads us in the renewal of all things.

But we do not live under false notions of idealism, thinking we will realize a utopian state of peace in this world before the return of Christ. Instead, we leave vengeance to God alone, trusting in the tension of his justice and mercy—living simultaneously as foreigners and strangers, and citizens and neighbors, working for the good as God leads us (Ephesians 2:10; Philippians 2:13).

Throughout history the Spirit has led men and women to follow in the footsteps of a crucified and risen Lamb, those who did not love their lives so much as to shrink from death (Revelation 12:11). May we, Christians all over the world, from every tradition and denomination, return to Jesus as the Prince of Peace—that the world may see nonviolence and enemy love as a central tenet of the Jesus movement once more.

May church pastors, ministry leaders, and all disciples of Jesus live and speak boldly, challenging the status quo of violence in the church. Pastors, don't worry about whether people will leave your church, get mad, or defame you—proclaim the truth of Jesus! For if we were trying to please people, we would no longer be servants of Christ (Galatians 1:10)! Rooted in our faith in the resurrection to come, let us cry in a united voice once again, "No blood but our own"—showing the world a narrow, third way.

Christ is a treasure worthy of our lives. His life, death, and resurrection are treasures. His peaceable kingdom and pathway of love are treasures. But all these treasures are held in our fragile and imperfect lives, which Paul called jars of clay (2 Corinthians 4:7). The beauty of Jesus' Sermon on the Mount, and the ethical standard therein, isn't something we can embody on our own—this is impossible for us. But all things are possible with God (Mark 10:27)! Through the power of Jesus' Spirit we will experience genuine transformation into people of peace who love their enemies and do not shrink from death, becoming salt and light to a dark and decaying world. We shall pray and overcome our cultural biases and prejudices; we will repent of implicit ideologies and nationalistic indoctrinations—and we will embody and proclaim the gospel message of Jesus' third way—the way of *peace*.

As individuals and as communities, we must create space for and wrestle with the life and teachings of Jesus as presented in the New Testament and by the early church. Christian peacebuilders embrace gospel nonviolence as part of their active commitment to transform the world and make the reign of God more visible—even while living in a world that remains under the shadow of sin, death, and the evil one.[28]

Amid these shadowy empires and principalities of darkness, the church exists as a beacon of light and hope, prophetically calling the world to repentance and peace, trusting God to be the purveyor of all life and death. As disciples we live as exilic outposts of peace, pilgrims bound up simultaneously in the hope and struggle of the already but not yet.

Our commitment to following and being formed by the Prince of Peace, loving our enemies, and creatively and actively making peace while rejecting violence will take more than we can muster ourselves. This cannot be done by human effort or strength alone; it will take the power of God. But it is *exactly* the power of God that raised Jesus from the dead that empowers us toward new life (Romans 6:4; 8:1)—a life of peaceful uncivil worship and nonviolent resistance of empire. In the words of Martin Luther King Jr. at his 1964 acceptance speech for the Nobel Peace Prize, it is "the unarmed truth and unconditional love that will have the final word in reality."[29]

Common Scriptural Questions about Christian Nonviolence

Inevitably, if you are going to talk about Christian nonviolence, you must deal with common objections, both scriptural and ethical. In my experience it has been a flip of a coin on whether an ethical or scriptural question arises when discussing Christian nonviolence for the first time. Here I will address some common scriptural questions in this section and some ethical ones in the next. You can also find a wealth of information about Christian nonviolence, including responses to many frequently asked questions, at the ecumenical site of Jesus Peace Collective.[1]

Before we dive in, it is important to remember that if we are not careful, we can find ways to make the Bible mean whatever we want it to mean. For instance, as historian Philip Jenkins writes in his book on violent biblical texts, "once a group or individual has decided that war is a holy and justified affair, they can seize on any available word or verse that consecrates the violence that is already taking place. Once someone has decided to do that, it scarcely matters what the text actually says."[2] This seems to be the case for the US sniper rifle manufacturer who had New Testament messages engraved on its scopes—including, ironically, passages like 1 John 1:7, which says to walk in the light as the blood of Jesus purifies us from all sin. (Even the sin of assassination, apparently.)[3] Similarly, this seemed to be the case for my neighbor who seized upon the biblical story of Samson killing Philistines with a jawbone to justify his own violence as sanctioned by God.

Many books about Christian nonviolence include frequently asked questions and common objections, and some books are devoted exclusively to this, but many of my readers may be unfamiliar with them—like I was for a long time in my faith.[4] Obviously, I will not respond to every question or objection to Christian nonviolence theology, but I hope to address several common ones that I have encountered along the way.

When I have a conversation about Christian nonviolence for the first time with someone, often one of the first objections is the killer at the door scenario: "You mean that if someone breaks into my house, I'm supposed to sit by and idly watch my spouse and children be raped and murdered?" I tell people that it *is* a valid question, and one that must be taken seriously—but it is best to set that question aside for the moment. *The best place to begin is to decide what is going to have authority for how we answer these questions.*

As Christians, it should be through Jesus as revealed in the Scriptures (1 Timothy 4:16). This means the best place to begin is with sorting out what Jesus taught and practiced on the subject. As this book seeks to establish, Jesus' life and teachings were consistently nonviolent. However, questions come up about a few things that Jesus said and did that seem to counter understanding him as nonviolent—so let's start there.

Didn't Jesus tell his disciples to go buy swords? (Luke 22)

In Luke 22:36–38, Jesus tells his disciples to go buy swords for his imminent arrest and conflict with the empire. "But now if you have a purse, take it, and also a bag; and if you don't have a sword, sell your cloak and buy one. It is written: 'And he was numbered with the transgressors'; and I tell you that this must be fulfilled in me. Yes, what is written about me is reaching its fulfillment" (vv. 36–37).[5] Of course, it is easy to see how a "plain" reading of this text might suggest that Jesus wants his disciples to arm themselves for the purposes of self-defense. If this is the case, then how could Jesus be against killing in all circumstances?

If this is the proper understanding of this passage, it *obviously* contradicts many of Jesus' other teachings.[6] However, I think the easiest way to understand this passage is in light of the context that Luke provides for his readers.

Immediately after Jesus' somewhat cryptic instruction to go buy swords, Luke writes that this happens so that he may be "numbered with the transgressors" and thus fulfill Isaiah's prophecy of the suffering servant (Isaiah 53:12). Whatever else is going on here, Luke indicates Jesus' inquiry to his band of non-soldier disciples having weapons is so that there could be a credible charge against him that he was leading a band of rebels against the empire. This scene concludes after the disciples, who apparently have not picked up on Jesus' intention, say they have two swords. Jesus breaks off the conversation by replying, "That's enough." The original language here is best understood to mean "Enough of this [foolish] conversation!" Clearly, two swords were not enough for any armed resistance against the empire. As one biblical scholar writes, "We can eliminate at once any idea that zealot sympathies are coming to expression with the commendation of the sword."[7]

Luke is making his audience aware that Jesus knew his time was coming to be dominated by empire and put to death. He tells his disciples to have at least a couple of weapons on them—but no more—*so the charge of insurrection could stick.* Only hours after this scene, Peter (who is identified in John's gospel) uses one of the two swords to defend his innocent rabbi. Immediately Jesus rebukes Peter and says this is no way to live in God's kingdom (Luke 22:51; see also Matthew 26:52). Jesus then continues his work of new creation by healing the man's wound inflicted by Peter's sword. To cement the point, Luke closes this scene with Jesus rhetorically asking why the religious leaders and officers have come to arrest him with weapons, as though he was leading a rebellion, military coup, or violent revolt. Matthew's gospel notes that this all happened so that the writings of the prophets might be fulfilled. Then all the disciples desert Jesus and flee for their lives (Matthew 26:56).

Didn't Jesus braid a whip and violently clear the temple? (John 2)

A common critique of understanding Jesus as nonviolent is the event known as the "temple cleansing," when John depicts Jesus braiding a whip, driving out livestock, and flipping over tables in the temple.

John clearly depicts Jesus as having righteous zeal, but is Jesus depicted as *violent*? Unlike the other gospel writers, John includes this scene near the opening of his account because he portrays Jesus in the prophetic lineage of Jeremiah. Jesus disrupts the temple system as he stages a prophetic rebuke of Israel's leaders—invoking memories of Jeremiah as Jesus proclaims they have turned his father's house into a den of robbers (John 2:13–22, compare Isaiah 56:7; Jeremiah 7:11). N. T. Wright calls this scene an "acted parable of judgment," saying it is best understood as an act of prophetic symbolism where Jesus reenacts and alludes to Jeremiah's sermon in Jeremiah 7:1–15.[8] In that sermon Jeremiah vehemently calls for repentance from Israel for stealing, murder, adultery, and idolatry.[9] (The debate about whether Jesus did this once during the Passion Week or multiple times in his ministry is irrelevant for our purposes.) Only in John's gospel, written several decades after the other gospels, is there mention of Jesus braiding a whip and using it to drive out the animals.[10]

Some claim that Jesus' action "most assuredly does not fit the profile of the ideological pacifist, for in truth it qualifies as forceful, even violent, resistance."[11] The temple cleansing "looks like a clear use of force and the resisting of evildoers," write scholars Paul Copan and Matthew Flannagan.[12]

It is true that violence can be notoriously tricky to define and defies easy categorization. "Despite its seemingly palpable core, violence is itself an ambiguous and elastic concept, . . . shading over from the direct use of force to cause bodily harm through the compelling or inducing of actions by direct threat of such force to partly or fully metaphorical notions of cultural or symbolic violence."[13] However, I think the Oxford English Dictionary definition of violence suffices for our purposes here: "Exercise of physical force so as to inflict injury on, or cause damage to, persons or property; action or conduct characterized by this; treatment or usage of tending to cause bodily injury or forcibly interfering with personal freedom."

As we take a closer look at Jesus' actions in the temple, it is undoubtedly a misstep to use this prophetic scene in the temple to justify violence of any kind. In John's gospel, the main point is not about whips, animals, and money changers—but rather the hollow and corrupt religious system that Jesus sets out to reenvision. He envisions that the temple and sacrificial system will no longer be corrupted, for his body will be the new temple. John explicitly says that Jesus' disciples remembered what he said in this scene after his resurrection and believed (John 2:20–22).

John's desire is to compel faith in the resurrection, not provide justification for Christians to be violent.

Jesus disrupts the temple system and incites fury from the temple leaders, and this scene teaches us something very important about following Jesus.

Being nonviolent doesn't mean being passive.

Jesus confronts, actively resists, and fights against evil. He is not timid. But he fights without employing violence against people, who are made in the image of God. His love of enemies compels him to confront and rebuke evil, to act, and to perform civil and religious disobedience for true righteousness. *May we have the courage to follow him.*

Why didn't John, Jesus, and Peter tell soldiers to quit their profession? (Luke 3, Matthew 8, Acts 10)

Some argue that if the New Testament meant for us to understand Jesus as nonviolent, then surely we would see that clearly in interactions with soldiers in the texts, as in the case of John the Baptist in Luke 3:14, Jesus commending the faith of the centurion in Matthew 8:5–13, and Peter with Cornelius, the Roman centurion, in Acts 10.

It is important to reemphasize the need to read the Bible through the lens of biblical theology, which focuses on the teachings and message of the biblical writers within their historical and literary contexts, and as it relates to the wider metanarrative of the whole of Scripture. This approach to reading the Bible can help safeguard us from imposing preconceived ideas or theological systems onto the text, and opens space for the Bible to speak on its own terms. It is also important that we don't lean too heavily on arguments made from silence in the Scriptures, since we can justify anything from such reasoning. For example, theologian and scholar Andy Alexis-Baker notes how we can draw fallacious conclusions by reading into what the text does not say:

> Since Jesus did not rebuke Pilate for being a governor of an occupying force, he must have sanctioned the Roman occupation and their right to exploit weaker nations, and by extension all colonial and military expansions. Since he did not ask Zacchaeus to leave his job as a tax collector, he must have approved of Roman tax collection and their right to drain resources from an area to the wealthy elite in Rome. Since Jesus did not admonish Pilate for murdering some Galileans in the midst of their sacrifices (Luke 13:3), he sanctioned police brutality and severe repressive measures. Since Jesus did not tell the judges at his own trial that they were wrong for their irregular court proceedings, he sanctions kangaroo courts and dictatorships today. Since Jesus did not reprove the centurion for owning slaves, he therefore condones slavery, even today. These arguments from silence can make Jesus to be the advocate of whatever we want.[14]

It is not fair to impose our own presuppositions onto the Scriptures if it is not the intent of the authors. Questions such as "If he wants us to live nonviolently, why did Jesus commend the soldier's faith instead of telling him to quit his profession?" put us "over" the text in that we want the passage to answer our specific questions, even if the writer may not have any desire to answer them, and instead intends to answer different questions.

A closer reading of these passages reveals that their primary purpose is very different from the questions we might bring to them. All three of these passages, one before the ministry of Jesus (John the Baptist in Luke 3), one during the ministry of Jesus (Jesus in Matthew 8), and one after the resurrection of Jesus (Peter in Acts 10), have very similar goals. They are announcing a single and radical truth: the kingdom of God is open to *all people*.

John the Baptist prepares the way for Jesus by proclaiming the coming kingdom and calling people to repentance (Luke 3:3–6). But how exactly is he preparing the way? His specific demand for repentance was for someone not to think that because they were an ethnic Israelite, they would inherently escape the coming wrath of God. John the Baptist says that God could raise up stones to fulfill his covenant with Abraham, a clear call to the inclusion of the Gentiles (Luke 3:7–8).

Luke highlights that tax collectors and soldiers came to be baptized, asking how they could be part of the coming salvation of God. Luke's primary purpose is not to spell out every relevant act of repentance for every person in the crowd, or his later readership, but rather to show that John prepared the way for the Lord by preaching about the inclusion of the Gentiles.[15] Luke specifically ties John's preparation with Isaiah's prophecy of the coming kingdom, that "all people will see God's salvation" (Luke 3:6; see also Isaiah 40:3–5).

During Jesus' own ministry, he comes across a soldier who recognizes his authority over all creation and asks for him to heal his servant (Matthew 8; Luke 7). Jesus is amazed at this man's faith. In Matthew's account, Jesus says that he has not seen such faith in Israel and that many will come from the east and west (referring to the Gentiles) to sit at Abraham's table in the kingdom of heaven—again, another clear allusion to ethnic inclusion in God's kingdom.

Even post-resurrection Peter needs divine intervention to see and understand this inclusive kingdom. God illuminates Peter when he visits him in a vision, commanding him not to call unclean what he has called clean—specifically Gentiles like Cornelius (Acts 10:9–23).

It is true that none of these interactions between soldiers and John the Baptist, Jesus, and Peter record them explicitly being told to quit their professions because of their incongruency with the kingdom of God—but that is not the point of these passages. The authors do not spell out every possible realm of repentance needed from every person in every situation.[16] Instead they are communicating that God's kingdom is breaking into the world to include all people groups and is not isolated to one ethnic nation.

It would behoove us to not force the Scriptures to speak from silence to support our own views, but rather allow the Bible to instruct us on its own terms. For a decisive word on how to treat our enemies, we should not turn to the few instances of soldiers in the New Testament when the author's aim was *not* to instruct on that subject, but rather to the teachings and life of Christ himself.

Aren't soldiers God's servants and the agents of his wrath? (Romans 13)

Romans 13:4 reads, "The one in authority is *God's servant for your good*. . . . for rulers do not bear the sword for no reason. They are *God's servants, agents of wrath to bring punishment on the wrongdoer*" (emphasis mine). At first glance it may seem that Paul is saying Christians can be God's servants as agents of his wrath against evil by utilizing violence. But when we look at the context of the passage and the flow of Paul's thought, we see that Paul is saying the *opposite*. The pagan rulers, *not Christians*, are God's agents of wrath.[17]

Just prior to this verse Paul says that the Christians in Rome are to bless those who persecute them, not repay evil for evil, and live at peace with everyone as long as it is on them. And they are not to take revenge, because it is God alone who is to avenge. Instead, Christians should feed their enemies when they are hungry and not exercise wrath to punish them (Romans 12:14–21). To use Romans 13 as a justification for why Christians can use violence and kill as members of the military or law enforcement cuts against the grain of what Paul says in Romans 12. Sure, Paul recognizes the existence of governments who utilize violence, but he says they are under the sovereign rule of God. He is not advocating anarchy or uprising against Rome, but he calls Christians to nonparticipation in systems of killing and violence.[18]

Simply put, *violence is the way of those outside of the kingdom of Jesus*. True, God sovereignly rules over the nations and their swords, but it is not the way of the Messiah—or his followers.

Peter also communicates a similar line of thought to Paul's in 1 Peter 2:11–25, where he tells the Christians, as foreigners and exiles (v. 11), to submit themselves to every human authority, *even if they are wicked* (v. 13)! Peter says that God sends authorities and governors to punish those who do wrong (v. 14), implying that Christians should not be doing any wrong. Instead, Christians are to "silence ignorant talk of foolish people because of their good behavior" (v. 15), even if they are enslaved by an evil and unjust slave owner, because "it is commendable if someone bears up under the pain of unjust suffering because they are conscious of God" (vv. 18–19).

Lord Jesus, this is a hard teaching; who can accept it?

Of course, this passage does not *condone* the practice of slavery—but this passage is an unbelievably high call of enemy love. Nor does it promote passivity—doing nothing in the face evil—but it calls for a different kind of resistance, and different kind of justice, one that is not retaliatory and does not repay evil for evil. Peter points to the nature of Jesus' nonviolent, nonretaliatory death as an example to imitate (vv. 21–23). He reminds us that this is our *why*—because we, like Jesus, entrust ourselves to the one who judges justly.

This is the heart of the matter. When we kill another human, we are ultimately taking judgment into our own hands to decide who should live or die. For Jesus followers this is simply not our judgment to make. Instead, we trust God to be the only just judge over life and death.

Isn't Jesus violent in the book of Revelation?

In Revelation, Jesus is depicted as a mighty warrior dripping with blood as he rides on a warhorse, with a sword coming out of his mouth, and treading the winepress of the fury of the wrath of God almighty (Revelation 19:11–15). This is an intense depiction of Jesus enacting justice on judgment day! The study of the end times is what scholars call eschatology, an area of theology concerned with the death, judgment, and final destiny of humanity.

John, in his final apocalyptic vision that we call Revelation, depicts a violent and just judgment by Jesus at the end of the age. However, his vision never encourages Jesus' followers to enact judgment or violence *themselves.*[19]

Instead, the book of Revelation calls Christians to bear nonviolent witness to the powers of the beast and resist them. This was written to the Babylon of John's context (Rome), but applies to every empire since—and yet to come. Their resistance is not by might, force, or violence—but by the blood of the Lamb and the word of their testimony (Revelation 12:11). John's vision was a manifesto to his audience: to not give in to fear of threats, the coercion of economic oppression, materialism, or greed—but to be willing to follow the slain and bloody Lamb, who is the King of the universe (Revelation 5:1–10).

May readers, through the ages, have ears to hear.

Isn't God violent—and doesn't God command war—in the Old Testament?

The Trappist monk Thomas Merton wrote, "It is of the very nature of the Bible to affront, perplex, and astonish the human mind. Hence the reader who opens the Bible must be prepared for disorientation, confusion, incomprehension, perhaps outrage."[20]

Understanding the violent depictions of God in the Scriptures (particularly in the Old Testament, but also in the New), may present some of the greatest challenges to our minds and hearts. Many who are committed to an orthodox view of the inspiration of Scripture, that it is all God-breathed (2 Timothy 3:16), have had difficulty understanding Jesus as a nonviolent peacemaker when considering the violent depictions of God in the Scriptures, such as when God instructed the Israelites to "not leave alive anything that breathes"—to kill every man, woman, child, and animal in Deuteronomy 20:16–17.

Many, as far back as the theologian Marcion of the second century, have attempted to resolve this tension by concluding the God of the Old Testament to be fundamentally different—perhaps even wicked—from the one depicted in Jesus. This view was widely considered heresy in Marcion's day and has continued to be seen as such throughout church history, but it is making a resurgence in our day—and you don't have to read the Bible for long to understand why.

Some modern scholars have gone so far as to say the violent depictions of God in the Old Testament are not divinely inspired, but instead are human fabrications, or self-projections, of the activity of God.[21] But I believe there are other ways to understand these texts.

Throughout church history, these Old Testament passages have been used to justify warfare and all types of killing, rationalizing that if God commanded the Israelites to kill their enemies, then Christians can do the same. Of course, this brings the teachings of Jesus, especially when viewed as the exact representation of God (Hebrews 1:3), into tension with these understandings of God.

In attempts to understand God's command to annihilate the Canaanites in the Old Testament (Deuteronomy 7), there have been many proposals to resolve this tension. These solutions include a range of ideas: the events never actually happened; those destroyed were wicked and deserved it; the command from God was occasional and thus not normative or prescriptive; the language used is hyperbolic and does not describe what actually happened; as a nation Israel must be able to defend itself in war; and many others.[22]

We must not dismiss these difficulties or quickly write them off, as they are genuinely difficult passages to reconcile.[23] And we must remember that while all Scripture is God-breathed and useful, it is not all equally relevant for us after the resurrection of Christ. We must be cautious of a flat reading of the Bible, where we take everything with equal weight. The New Testament authors considered Jesus the fulfillment of the previous covenant, while ushering in a new one. Therefore, they viewed all Scripture in light of him, creating a Christ-centered approach to understand the diverse witness of Scripture.

As New Testament scholar Richard Hays has said, "The cross and resurrection define the interpretive lens through which Scripture as a whole is to be read."[24] This means that God has progressively revealed himself in Scripture, and throughout history—leading to the culmination of divine revelation in Jesus. While Jesus does not reveal every *possible* thing about God, he reveals all we need to know to live in shalom—with God and with other people.[25]

Although we view all the Scriptures through the person and work of Jesus, some presentations of God in the Old Testament undoubtedly pose moral dilemmas to our view of God. However, Paul, along with other New Testament authors, seems to have no moral conflict with relegating justice and wrath to God alone while emphatically saying that our role as Christians is to love our enemies and not exact revenge (e.g., Romans 12:19).

Isaiah observed that the clay has no right to interrogate the potter (Isaiah 45:9). Job mistakenly spoke of things too wonderful for him to know (Job 42:3). David said he didn't want to concern himself with great matters that were too wonderful for him (Psalm 131:1). And Paul said that we, as human beings, should not talk back to God (Romans 9:20). While these answers may not satisfy, great humility is required because now we only see as in a glass darkly (1 Corinthians 13:12), and as Old Testament scholars Richard Hess and Elmer Martens have said on the subject, "the mystery of God's operations are beyond human comprehension."[26] Ronald Sider captures this tension well: "Perhaps this side of eternity, we will never have an adequate answer to the question of violence in the Old Testament. But that lack of clarity in no way leaves uncertain what faithful disciples of Jesus should believe and do. If God's final revelation, the eternal Son of God, calls his disciples to love their enemies, we must obey."[27]

Common Ethical Questions about Christian Nonviolence

Beyond questions of how to understand the Scriptures considering Jesus' nonviolence, ethical questions arise as well. Can I truly love my neighbor if she is killed when I could have done something about it? Would God consider employing violence against a greater evil a necessary (and therefore lesser) evil? If all Christians were pacifists, wouldn't evil run rampant in the world? Is it hypocritical for a Christian pacifist to call the police for protection? And many, many others.

Blaise Pascal said, "Men never do evil so completely and cheerfully as when they do it from religious conviction." Violence, whether eschatological or otherwise, is to be the purview of God alone, as we are commanded to leave room for God's wrath (Romans 12:19). Jesus' followers are not to employ violence to exercise their will or preserve their lives; rather, they are to love their enemies and entrust themselves to

God, who judges justly (1 Peter 2:23). Christian nonviolence understandably raises many scriptural and ethical questions—not least because it has not been seriously considered by most Christians in America, or elsewhere for that matter. However, a deep consideration of the Scriptures reveals that Jesus taught and lived a nonviolent life and expected his followers to do the same.

Walter Wink beautifully articulates one of the primary reasons we can have a hard time accepting Jesus at his word. It doesn't concern our interpretations of Scripture—but whether we think we can *actually do it*. Wink says that not many people have aspired to Jesus' third way "because it has been presented to them as absolute pacifism, a life-commitment to nonviolence in principle, without exceptions. They are neither sure that they can hold fast to its principle in every situation nor sure that they have the saintliness to overcome their own inner violence." He rightly points out that we know just how weak we are and that we will likely fail, but God is gracious and forgiving and helps us get back up when we fall. "Seen in this light, Jesus' Third Way is not an insuperable counsel to perfection attainable only by the few. It is simply the right way to live, and can be pursued by many. *The more who attempt it, the more mutual support there will be in following it.*"[1]

Christian nonviolence and peacemaking are not meant to be seen as an ethical option sitting alongside other ethical options such as just war perspectives—rather, Christian pacifism is best understood as a practice, a way of life, a heart posture. It is an ongoing practice of communal life that envisions Christian discipleship as a transformed life of love—enabled and empowered by the Spirit of Christ.[2]

The killer at the door—isn't Christian pacifism just being passive?

The question of the killer at the door is undoubtedly one of the most common questions that I hear from people in discussions of Christian enemy love. It goes something like this: "You mean that to love my enemies means watching my family be raped and killed by the person who breaks into my home, and do *nothing*?" Or as C. S. Lewis put it, "Does anyone suppose . . . that if a homicidal maniac, attempting to murder a third party, tried to knock me out of the way, I must stand aside and let him get his victim?"[3] This logic goes at least as far back as Ambrose of Milan, a Christian leader of the fourth century (after the time of Constantine): "He who does not keep harm off a friend, if he can, is as much in fault as he who causes it."[4]

I find it interesting that this response is typically from men, revealing where our minds and hearts can immediately go when confronted with the idea of loving our enemies. Jesus says, "Love your enemies," and many respond, "You want me to watch my family be murdered!?" It may seem like an irrational jump—but it is completely understandable. Who wants to be led like a sheep to the slaughter? This is especially the case when we are inundated with the message that only the strong survive! We must take this kind of objection seriously because it is not just a hypothetical potentiality. However, doing nothing is *not* Christian nonviolence.

Christian pacifism is *not* passive.

Today, the term *pacifism* carries the meaning of opposition to war or an attitude of nonresistance.[5] However, the word is derived from the Latin word *pacific*, which means peace-making (*paci* comes from *pax*, meaning "peace," and *ficus* means "making").[6] This is not the same thing as being *passive*. Being passive denotes permitting things to happen and not acting.[7]

In this sense Jesus was certainly *not* passive. As Gandhi said, Jesus was "the most active resister known to history."[8] Jesus did not sit idly by watching evil and doing nothing. No, love compelled him to actively resist evil—*nonviolently*. Jesus did not say that we should love our enemies and pray for them unless they happen to threaten us or our loved ones, in which case we could kill them.

In the parable of the good Samaritan, Jesus confronts the ethnic and racial discrimination of the religious leader who wanted to justify bigotry (Luke 10:25–37). This story reveals that in Jesus' kingdom, those we deem "other," or "enemy," are in actuality *our neighbors*. So the argument that we can kill our enemy to protect and love our neighbor just doesn't work. In Jesus' kingdom we don't have enemies, we only have neighbors—so if we kill our enemy, we have killed our neighbor.

This sounds good in theory, but of course I can't say with certainty what I *would* do in a threatening situation. I know my imagination is often conditioned to only two options though: *kill or be killed*. Considering the new creation that began with Jesus and his resurrection, there are a myriad of ways we could plan to actively resist evil, restoring justice and love in the world without using violence. But in truth, I often think of violence as a first resort.

John Howard Yoder's book *What Would You Do?*, devoted exclusively to the topic of a pacifist facing danger, raises an excellent point: when Christians consider nonviolence, it is not simply an ethical stance we want to be consistent with, or rules we don't want to break—rather, Christian nonviolence is a gracious privilege we want to share with others created in the image of God. We believe that God intervenes in the lives of selfish creatures to change them, and often does so through his image bearers. When is my conviction tested more than when I am invited to act toward an aggressor as though there can be no change of heart for them?[9]

In every instance in the New Testament that portrays a physical threat, either to Jesus or his followers, there is no clear allowance to use violence to defend oneself. Yet there is ample evidence that we are not to resist evil with evil, but instead turn the other cheek, go the extra mile, and repay evil with good (Matthew 5:38–48; Romans 12:17; 1 Peter 3:9). And let's face it: repaying evil with good is an *active* resistance. Many passages place great value on suffering when wrongfully attacked or for doing good (1 Peter 2:11; 3:13–18).[10] Though it may seem unloving or cowardly toward those being threatened to not act violently toward the (hypothetical) homicidal maniac at the door, it ultimately *reveals who I believe rules over life and death*.

Yes, Jesus has all authority in heaven and on earth, but this is not an excuse for passivity. Jesus' peacemaking and resistance of evil takes great faith, self-control, discipline, and *new-creation-prophetic-imagination*. As an example of such an imagination, I once heard a story of a family staying at a motel that was broken into at gunpoint, with the assailants screaming to give them money. Calmly and decisively, the mother began singing "Jesus Loves Me," and she walked with arms wide open toward her assailants. They freaked out (understandably) and yelled at the top of their lungs, "These are some of those Jesus freaks!" as they ran out of the room.

Of course, we are not guaranteed such outcomes, but we *can* start allowing ourselves, and our imaginations, to be formed and informed by the Spirit of Jesus to show us alternatives to violence. Violence is the unimaginative broad road that leads to further violence and destruction—but Jesus invites us down a narrower path.

Evils like Hitler—if everyone was pacifist, wouldn't evil run rampant?

"What about Adolf Hitler?" is probably the second-most common question I hear in first-time conversations about Christian nonviolence.[11] This is understandable, as Hitler wreaked havoc and death on an almost unimaginable scale. Tragically, it is not unimaginable, because it happened.

And things like it have happened throughout human history, *repeatedly*.

What Walter Wink calls the "domination system" arose in the Middle East sometime between 4000 and 3000 BCE. Before this time, archaeological evidence shows there were many peaceful civilizations—cities with no walls, no armies, no weapons for battle. After 3000 BCE, however, warfare proliferates the archaeological evidence dramatically.[12]

Hitler's name is paradigmatic in arguments against pacifism, as it has come to represent the argument that Christian pacifism simply defies common sense. Deitrich Bonhoeffer's name is also frequently named in conjunction with the Hitler question. Bonhoeffer was a Christian pastor and prophetic theologian who reportedly took part in an assassination plot on Hitler's life that was unsuccessful (though Bonhoeffer's involvement in the assassination attempt is debated and remains unclear).[13] Bonhoeffer's example is often considered as the commonsense response to such atrocities as Hitler and reveals the limits of Christian pacifism—people like Hitler must be ended!

The simplicity of encoding this argument in a single word like "Hitler" leads to what philosopher Robert Brimlow called the "Hitlerization of politics." This is how the argument often goes:

1. There is evil in the world, and so-and-so is an evildoer whose evil actions harm or kill innocents.
2. These evil actions must be stopped: it is our moral and religious obligation to try to stop evil from spreading further and harming or killing more innocent people.
3. There are no nonviolent means or methodologies that will be effective in stopping the evil, since it is relentless and ruthless.
4. Therefore, an effective violent methodology is our only available alternative to satisfy our moral obligation.
5. So, we ought to engage in whatever violent actions necessary to stop the evil from spreading further.[14]

But the common sense of "Hitlerization" is not the only consideration, because Jesus often *defies* common sense. He sends us out as sheep among wolves, not as conquering soldiers (Matthew 10:16). Nor does he promise that we will overcome evil in a temporal, physical sense. No, he promised the opposite, that we will be persecuted and hated when we follow him (John 15:18–20). It is God's sovereign prerogative to rule over the nations and their leaders, including their swords (Romans 13:1–5). Jesus followers are not to participate in the process of wielding the sword, but instead are to call out evil, help those who are oppressed and suffering, and pray for the leaders of nations that we may live lives of peace (1 Timothy 2:1–4).

When was the last time you prayed for world leaders, especially the ones you think are evil, that there may be peace?

I once had the opportunity to mentor a young Christian man who was considering enlisting in the military because he was struggling to find a viable career path. Military enlistment seemed like a good fit because they would accept him, it came with good pay and benefits, and it was full of travel and adventure. What more could a young single guy want?

At the time, as a church we were not explicitly pacifist, and he had never considered the nonviolent teachings of Jesus before. Through several conversations together over a period of a few months, I invited him to wrestle with what Jesus might want him to do regarding enlistment. After he wrestled with the Lord in Scripture, prayer, and community, he concluded that as a Christian he could not willingly take a job that might require him to kill someone. However, he still wanted to use his talents and gifts to serve others, so he decided to attempt to become an aviation survival technician in the US Coast Guard. ASTs are noncombatant elite military personnel in the Coast Guard. Though they are not technically special forces, they are elite first responders, specialized rescue swimmers, primarily focused on search and rescue operations, who have the highest degree of physical and mental fitness. These are the guys who jump out of helicopters to save people at sea, in floods, and on cliffside rescues. I was proud of his decision, and personally grateful when he brought his skills to help after our region experienced devastating flooding from Hurricane Helene in 2024.

The desire to vanquish evil with violence is often motivated by a sincere love for those who are suffering and oppressed. No doubt this love beats with the heart of God. As Christians we are not called primarily to nonviolence, nor to be nonviolent actors in the world, as though they were isolated principles—instead we are called to *follow Christ.* For instance, Gandhi was an incredible nonviolent activist in the world and brought about great social change for good, but he was not a Christian.[15] As followers of Christ, we are to integrate Jesus' call to nonviolence with caring for the marginalized in a holistic practice of discipleship.

As we follow Jesus in a holistic approach of discipleship, we must do so with humility, not becoming haughty or arrogant in our nonviolent stances and convictions and recognizing that any of us is capable of evils far greater than we tend to think. This means we humbly leave the execution of justice in God's hands, for we are all wicked and have gone astray like sheep (1 Peter 2:25). In a powerful display of this type of humility, Primo Levi, a survivor of the Holocaust, wrote about his captors in Auschwitz:

> They were not monsters. I didn't see a single monster in my time in the camp. Instead I saw people like you and I who were acting in that way because there was Fascism, Nazism in Germany. Were some form of Fascism or Nazism to return, there would be people, like us, who would act in the same way, everywhere. And the same goes for the victims.[16]

Some argue that if all Christians were pacifists, evil would run rampant in the world—and there would be no more Christians! This is an ancient argument leveled at Origen of the second century by the Roman pagan Celsus, who said, "For if all were to do the same as you [Christians] . . . the affairs of the earth would fall into the hands of the wildest and most lawless barbarians."[17] As King Solomon said, there is nothing new under the sun. But Origen's defense was sound: he argued that any persecution that comes on Christians is sovereignly ruled over by God, that Christ has overcome the world, and persecution lasts only as long as God allows it. Origen believed that God would not allow the Christian faith or the church to be vanquished by evil.

Origen wrote this during a time of persecution. Even though Christianity was illegal and Roman officials often martyred Christians, the faith flourished and spread throughout the Roman Empire. When this question is raised about figures like Hitler and the pervasiveness of evil in the world, disciples of Jesus must respond with trust and faith in God, even if it costs us our lives, because we believe, along with the apostle Paul, that *to die is gain* (Philippians 1:21).

What about the police—aren't pacifists just getting others to do their dirty work for them?

In 2015 I was an associate pastor for a church in Columbia, South Carolina, when a mass shooting at Emanuel AME Church occurred a couple of hours away in Charleston. A twenty-one-year-old white supremacist shot and killed nine Black church members and clergy after joining their weekly Bible study for nearly an hour. He opened fire while they prayed with their eyes shut. He was sentenced to death in 2017 and now sits on death row awaiting execution.[18]

Mass shootings have tragically become commonplace in America, but this one hit especially close to home because of its proximity to our church and the fact that I was a pastor in a predominately Black church. Many of the victims' family members amazingly offered public forgiveness at the man's bond hearing. Concurrently, our church decided to increase its security, hire police to patrol during services, and provide training to the congregation for active shooter scenarios.

During one such training, a church member who was an active police officer at the time spoke to the congregation from the stage about active shooter scenarios and coldly said, "If there is an active shooter situation here, some of you are going to die, and you simply need to be ready for that." During this active shooter drill, my young child, along with all the other children of the church, was marched across the street without their parents to the adjacent school building. My child was barely a year old.

My wife and I felt especially uncomfortable with our one-year-old being taken across the street without us in an active shooter drill scenario. Although I didn't necessarily have nonviolent convictions expressly formulated at that time, I remember feeling uneasy as the usher team ordered new walkie-talkie equipment and put many members who carried firearms to church on the team. Looking back, I wish there had been some conversation among the leadership of the church to sort through how to best respond to threats as we gathered as a community of Christians. Perhaps this would have surfaced how to best appropriate Jesus' teachings on how to love our enemies. Instead I think it was the "common sense" and fleshly knee-jerk reaction that prevailed.

Christian pacifists are accused of not loving their neighbors if they are unwilling to meet evil with violence. Critics say that Christian pacifists have a naive, unrealistic, and overly optimistic view of human nature, and that they are selfish cowards, freeloading off a society they aren't willing to get their hands dirty to protect. That they benefit from a society others died to create. That they are dishonoring those who gave up their lives so we can be free.[19]

I am sincerely thankful for many of the freedoms I have living in the United States, but Jesus followers are mistaken if we think freedom is reduced to things like the freedom to assemble, freedom of speech and religion, freedom to bear arms, and the right to petition the government. True freedom, Jesus taught, is that we are free from the power of sin and death (John 8:31–36). My Christian brothers and sisters in China may not possess the same societal and political freedoms that I do, yet in Christ they are absolutely free.

Today, policing in America has become increasingly militarized—and politicized. Policing is complex and cannot simply be reduced to a single issue or even set of issues. Police officers play a myriad of roles in a society that vary across societies—and every society requires some function of policing.[20] The question is, how should that policing to be done?

Christian pacifists have different views about Christian involvement in law enforcement and are at times particularly ambivalent on the matter. This challenge is not simply because of the difficulty of living up to the ethical ideals of Jesus' kingdom, which is hard enough, but because it intersects with how the Christian community understands itself to exist among the societies of the world—the tension of living in the "already but not yet" reality of the kingdom as we know it currently.[21]

As we live in this tension, however, we must recognize that killing is simply not the way of Jesus. Christians are never to voluntarily engage in a vocational role in society that could require them to kill. This has direct implications for military and law enforcement, as well as other vocations such as judges who sentence criminals to the death penalty, executioners, or perhaps even doctors who could one day be required by law to kill unborn babies or patients via assisted suicide.[22]

However, killing another person made in the image of God is not the only thing in view—there are issues of allegiance and integrity of purpose as well in some vocations that are at odds with Jesus' kingdom. While it is true that police officers may go their entire career without ever firing their weapon, it has been said, "Anyone who rules out categorically firing a gun in the course of their work should not enter police work in the first place."[23] A police officer who was visiting our church once confided in me that if they took Jesus' teachings seriously and decided they would not kill, they would be jeopardizing their partner's life, who would be counting on them to protect them in the line of fire. Therefore, it would be unethical to continue to be a police officer if he could not kill someone.

But what about calling the police if your life, or someone else's life, is threatened? Can pacifists rely on nonpacifists to serve as police officers for their protection? It's one thing to not *be* a police officer, but can they *utilize* the police for themselves or others? And if they do, isn't that just getting someone else to do their "dirty work?" To have someone else do for them what they are unwilling to do themselves? Isn't this hypocrisy, plain and simple?

This is a fair and honest question. And any response to it must be incredibly nuanced.

Paul's explanation to the Christians in Rome about the role of the state and its violence is that God sovereignly rules over it and uses it to "punish the wrongdoer" (Romans 13:4). While I am admittedly reading between the lines, it seems that when Paul's life was in danger from an angry mob, he was himself rescued by the hands of the military/police and their swords in Acts 21–23. While there is no indication that he called for their help, Paul certainly doesn't argue about it having happened.

While he didn't employ violence through others, he does use his privileged status as a Roman citizen to *escape* violence and being flogged, calling upon the laws of the land to protect him (Acts 22:25–29). However, there is no record of Paul, or any other Christian in the New Testament, telling the military/police to harm someone else in order to protect themselves—even if their lives, or the lives of their loved ones, were in danger.

Obviously, the Scriptures do not parse out all possible vocational roles for Christians in every cultural context throughout human history. We must discern and seek wisdom about these complex questions, for it is impossible to predict for certain what any one of us would do in a given situation until we are in it. Honestly, if I found myself in the situation my pastor friend in New York City did—he came across a man beating a woman in the street and so my friend hit the man with a stick and broke his arm—I hope I would have the restraint to only break the assailant's arm!

That being said, it seems clear that a Christian should not take vocational roles that could *require* them to kill, which in America would include law enforcement. Whether a Christian should call the police so that they can "punish the wrongdoer," potentially killing them, is a very difficult question—and should not be answered hastily. But our lack of imagination and intentionality often prohibits us from finding alternatives to violence. The choice is rarely binary—dial 911 or die. Those who follow the Prince of Peace have their theology rooted in the death and resurrection of Christ, which "reveals how God deals with evil; and is the only valid starting point for Christian pacifism or nonresistance."[24]

Group Reflection Questions

This guide is designed for small groups who have read *The Unarmed Truth* or are reading it together.

Chapter 1: A War on Mars: A Southern Pastor's (Reluctant) Journey into Nonviolence

- What interested you in reading this book?
- What has your experience been like up to this point regarding violence and your faith?
- Is there anything about the author's experience that resonates with you personally?
- Have you ever intentionally considered the subject of Christian nonviolence before? Why or why not?

Chapter 2: But I Tell You: Jesus' Vision of Enemy Love

- How do you see the culture of violence play out in the world around you? How do you see violence in *yourself*?

- Have you understood Jesus' teaching in the Sermon on the Mount to mean that his followers should be nonviolent? If not, how have you understood that passage?
- Have you thought some forms of violence are acceptable for a Christian, and some not? What has that been based on?
- Have you understood Jesus' call to love our enemies to be central to what it means to follow him? Why or why not?
- What might it look like for you to love people more indiscriminately and unconditionally as God does (Matthew 5:45) right now? Is there a person (or people) whom you find it difficult to do this with? If so, consider praying for that person (or people) right now (Matthew 5:44).

Chapter 3: Subversive Confrontation: Jesus and the Powers

- What do you notice most when reading about the power struggle between Jesus and Pilate in John 18–19?
- How might you grasp for worldly power in your life?
- What might it look like for you to employ nonviolent resistance and ultimately trust God over life and death, as Jesus did?
- In what ways do you see the inversion of right and wrong in you and around you?
- If "God looks like Jesus," what truths of God do you find inconvenient or troubling right now? What truths do you find inspiring and filled with hope?

Chapter 4: A Cosmic War: The Apostles Follow Jesus into Nonviolent Battle

- How has this chapter helped you view the writings of the New Testament authors as proclaiming a nonviolent and peaceable kingdom of Jesus?
- What new themes, links, and connections do you think you will see differently as you read the New Testament now?
- What Scriptures in the New Testament seem contrary to the understanding presented in this chapter?
- Jesus transformed Paul's violent religious zeal into nonviolent peacemaking. What relevance does this observation have for you?

Chapter 5: Swords into Plowshares: The Early Church Witness to the Sanctity of Life

- How is the early church's understanding of Jesus' teachings around violence and the sanctity of life different from or similar to your own?
- What do you think motivated the early Christians to take such stances in their context?
- What would it look like for you to have a similarly consistent stance about the sanctity of life as the early church?
- Consider asking God to reveal a small step forward you can take.

Chapter 6: A Marriage of Two Kingdoms: A Seismic Shift

- How can you see the effects of the "marriage of two kingdoms" in your context and in your faith?
- How have Augustine's ideas about the "two cities" (the separation of the Christian following Jesus in two spheres—public and private) affected your understanding of following Jesus personally?
- Why do you think many Western Christians have not heard much about this part of church history?

Chapter 7: No Blood but Our Own: The Historic Peace Churches

- What emotions rise in you as you read this chapter? Why do you think those feelings arise in you?
- If you do not come from a historic peace tradition, what do you think you can learn from these streams throughout history?
- If you do come from a historic peace tradition, in what ways might Jesus be calling you deeper into his gospel of peace in the world?
- How do you feel when you read about martyrs who died for their faith throughout history and did not retaliate or seek revenge on their assailants? How do you feel about so many of these martyrs having been killed by others who profess Christ?

Chapter 8: One Nation Under God: Christian Nationalism in the United States

- Do you believe that America is a Christian nation, specially chosen by God for his purposes? Why or why not?
- How do US Christians tend to overlook the dark underbelly of their nation's past? No matter where we live, how can we be more honest about our nation's weaknesses and its strengths?
- In what ways have you believed that "might makes right"? Where has that come from?

Chapter 9: God and Guns: America and the Myth of Redemptive Violence

- In what ways do you find that you enjoy violence?
- How do you see the myth of redemptive violence ideology fueled by culture and society? How can it take root in you personally?
- What might it look like for you, your family, and your community to resist Christian nationalism and the myth of redemptive violence?

Chapter 10: Let God Sort 'Em Out: A Southern Congregation's (Reluctant) Journey into Nonviolence and Hope for a New World

- In what ways might Jesus be challenging your own cultural and religious assumptions?
- What might it look like for you to become more of a peacemaker in your life right now?

- How do you feel about the US Second Amendment and the "right" to own guns as a Christian?
- Do you notice any ways you have been shaped by your context that are opposed to the gospel of Jesus?

Chapter 11: Exilic Outposts: Subversive Resistance and Uncivil Worship

- What creative ways might Jesus be calling you toward peace in your life and the world?
- Is there an "enemy" in your life you can invite to your table for a meal of reconciliation? (Psalm 23:5)
- Where do you feel tension or resistance to where Jesus might be inviting you?
- In addition to possible political activism, what are some other ways you can be a peacemaker in your home, church, neighborhood, workplace, and community?

Common Scriptural Questions about Christian Nonviolence

- Which of these common scriptural questions do you find most difficult? Why?
- Are there other scriptural questions you have that are not covered here?
- How do you feel when you consider that we may never fully comprehend the violent depictions of God in the Scriptures?

Common Ethical Questions about Christian Nonviolence

- Which of these common ethical questions do you find most difficult? Why?
- Are there other ethical questions you have that are not covered here?
- What thoughts or reactions arise when you consider the possibility that our hesitation toward Jesus' third way of nonviolence may stem less from how we interpret Scripture and more from our own sense of what is or isn't possible?

Acknowledgments

I would like to thank all the family, friends, and colleagues who have believed in me and this project, along with those who helped it come to fruition. Thank you to the team at Herald Press, particularly the acquisitions editor Sara Versluis. Instrumental in this journey was the McAfee School of Theology at Mercer University, in particular Dr. David G. Garber and Dr. Heidi Miller, who pushed me to make my doctoral thesis better, from which this book was born.

I would also like to thank those who provided critical feedback on the book during the development process, such as Jeff Hickman, Alexander and Erin Lange, Katie Ottenweller, Dr. David C. Cramer, Dr. Douglas A. Jacoby, and Dr. David P. Gushee. This has been done alongside the beautiful network of micro churches and their leadership team in western North Carolina, who have played an indispensable role and provided the backbone for this project.

Finally, I would like to send a heartfelt and special thanks to my wife and two sons, without whose support and encouragement this could not have happened, along with so many other things in my life—I love you.

Notes

Preface

1 Nonviolence as Christian discipleship is one aspect of a broader spectrum of thought and theology within Christian nonviolence. For a treatment of this spectrum, see David C. Cramer and Myles Werntz, *A Field Guide to Christian Nonviolence: Key Thinkers, Activists, and Movements for the Gospel of Peace* (Baker Academic, 2022).

Chapter 1

1 Kristin Kobes Du Mez gives this Jesus a full treatment in her book *Jesus and John Wayne: How White Evangelicals Corrupted a Faith and Fractured a Nation* (Liveright Publishing, 2021), 5.

2 This iconic quote is from hip-hop artist André 3000 of Outkast as they accepted their best new artist Source award in 1995. See also Esau McCaulley, *Reading While Black: African American Biblical Interpretation as an Exercise in Hope* (InterVarsity Press, 2020), 4.

3 Du Mez, *Jesus and John Wayne*, 3–4.

4 Interestingly, the US Marine recruitment officer at that time was more than eager to overlook my drug addiction and find a way around my drug screening to get me to sign up and ship off to basic training.

5 Throughout this book I may use colloquial masculine pronouns (he/him/his) for God simply out of convenience and familiarity. I believe Jesus referred to God with male pronouns as an accommodation in his patriarchal context, and that both male and female are made equally as image bearers in the Genesis creation account. Thus, my usage is not to be confused with patriarchy, or a "male" view of God. God does not have a penis and I'm just as comfortable referring to God as "she;" however, God is neither male nor female, for God is Spirit (John 4:24). Because of the personal and relational nature of God, I chose not to employ the English pronoun *it* for any aspect of the triune God.

6 Eventually I got rid of my gun when I got married, as my wife wasn't comfortable having a handgun in our home.

7 I use the traditional terminology of "Old" and "New" Testaments to refer to the Hebrew Scriptures along with the Christian writings, as opposed to "First" and "Second" Testaments or something similar. I do this out of familiarity and tradition, but I recognize and affirm the continuity between the "Old" and "New."

Chapter 2

1 See Preston Sprinkle, *Nonviolence: The Revolutionary Way of Jesus* (David C Cook, 2021), 117.

2 Jesse P. Nickel, *A Revolutionary Jesus: Violence and Peacemaking in the Kingdom of God* (Fortress Press, 2024), 9.

3 André Trocmé, *Jesus and the Nonviolent Revolution*, 2nd ed., ed. Charles E. Moore (Plough Publishing, 2003), xix.

4 Craig G. Bartholomew and Michael W. Goheen, *The Drama of Scripture: Finding Our Place in the Biblical Story,* 3rd ed. (Baker Academic, 2024), xxiii.

5 I follow in Greg Boyd's footsteps in a canonical approach and theological interpretation of Scripture. See Gregory A. Boyd with M. Scott Boren, *God Looks Like Jesus: A Renewed Approach to Understanding God* (Herald Press, 2025). See also Michael J. Gorman, *Scripture and Its Interpretation: A Global, Ecumenical Introduction to the Bible* (Baker Academic, 2017); Kevin J. Vanhoozer, *Mere Christian Hermeneutics: Transfiguring What It Means to Read the Bible Theologically* (Zondervan Academic, 2024); and Daniel J. Treier, *Introducing Theological Interpretation of Scripture: Recovering a Christian Practice* (Baker Academic, 2008).

6 Graeme Goldsworthy, *Christ-Centered Biblical Theology: Hermeneutical Foundations and Principles* (IVP Academic, 2012), 150.

7 David P. Gushee and Glen H. Stassen, *Kingdom Ethics: Following Jesus in Contemporary Context*, 2nd ed. (Wm. B. Eerdmans, 2016), 62.

8 Bartholomew and Goheen, *Drama of Scripture*, xxiv.

9 See Scot McKnight, *The Bible Is Not Enough: Imagination and Making Peace in the Modern World* (Fortress Press, 2023); and Walter Brueggemann, *The Prophetic Imagination: 40th ann. ed.* (Fortress Press, 2018).

10 Gregory A. Boyd, *Crucifixion of the Warrior God: Interpreting the Old Testament's Violent Portraits of God in Light of the Cross*, vol. 1 (Fortress Press, 2017), 34.

11 George Kalantzis, *Caesar and the Lamb: Early Christian Attitudes on War and Military Service* (Cascade Books, 2012), 59.

12 Craig M. Watts, *Disciple of Peace: Alexander Campbell on Pacifism, Violence, and the State* (Doulos Christou Press, 2005), 121.

13 Terrence J. Rynne, "Jesus and Nonviolence: Scriptural Evidence," in *Choosing Peace: The Catholic Church Returns to Gospel Nonviolence*, ed. Marie Dennis (Orbis, 2018), 80.

14 See Jeremy Gabrielson, *Paul's Non-Violent Gospel: The Theological Politics of Peace in Paul's Life and Letters* (Pickwick Publications, 2013), 2–4.

15 Though some of Jesus' teachings in the Sermon on the Mount are hyperbolic, such as cutting off one's hand (Matthew 5:29-30), it is clear his teaching on enemy love is not hyperbole but is meant to be taken literally because of his own embodiment of it, along with that of his apostles and the early church.

16 Warren Carter, "The Gospel of Matthew" in *A Postcolonial Commentary on the New Testament Writing*, ed. Fernando F. Segovia and R. S. Sugirtharajah (Bloomsbury Publishing, 2009), 72–73.

17 Some, such as N. T. Wright, categorize them as five antitheses. See N. T. Wright, *Jesus and the Victory of God: Christian Origins and the Question of God*, vol. 2 (Fortress Press, 1996), 289.
18 Kenneth L. Barker and John R. Kohlenberger III, *The Expositor's Bible Commentary, Abridged Edition: New Testament* (Zondervan, 1994), 30.
19 Barker and Kohlenberger, *Expositor's Bible Commentary*, 30. See also Craig S. Keener, *The IVP Bible Background Commentary, New Testament*, 2d ed. (IVP Academic, 2014), 60.
20 Wright, *Victory of God*, 290.
21 As scholar and early church professor Paul T. Sloan notes, "Resurrected, Jesus initiates and embodies the restoration and renewed covenant he formerly heralded, and with his acquired authority over heaven and earth, he commissions his disciples to summon Israel and the nations to allegiance to him and his interpretation of the Law as the world's appointed ruler and judge." Paul T. Sloan, *Jesus and the Law of Moses: The Gospels and the Restoration of Israel within First-Century Judaism* (Baker Academic, 2025), 214.
22 See Hosea 1:5–7, 12:1; Micah 5:10–11; Amos 9:11–15; Isaiah 22:5–11, 30:1–3, 31:1–5, etc. Preston Sprinkle helpfully notes that the Old Testament begins with peace set forth as the ideal in the Genesis creation account, and "the prophets proclaim a message that in general moves *away from violence* and *toward peace*." The Old Testament then ends longing for peace that "stitches together the seemingly contradictory portraits of violence in the Old Testament and nonviolence in the New." Sprinkle, *Nonviolence*, 113. Emphasis in the original.

Chapter 3

1 Gerald L. Borchert, *John 12–21*, vol. 25B, The New American Commentary (Broadman & Holman, 2002), 224.
2 Richard Rohr and Andreas Ebert, *The Enneagram: A Christian Perspective* (Crossroad Publishing, 2016), 244.
3 E.g., see the seven "I am" statements in John's gospel (6:35; 8:12; 10:7, 11; 11:25; 14:6; 15:1) as Jesus proclaims the reality that "God looks like Jesus."
4 Lecrae, "Truth," track 7 on *Rebel*, 2006. Genius, https://genius.com/Lecrae-truth-lyrics (accessed April 17, 2025).
5 "If you look at human life on its own, it looks like death reigns, like all of human government, for its power depends upon the ability to kill. There is no human government that doesn't rest on the power to kill." Dallas Willard, "Your Kingdom and God's Kingdom," February 18, 2010, in *The Dallas Willard Podcast*, episode 54, https://open.spotify.com/episode/50fpsacIGHj7PjqROIP3az.
6 Gerald L. Sittser, *Resilient Faith: How the Early Christian "Third Way" Changed the World* (Brazos, 2019), 102.

Chapter 4

1 See, e.g., Matthew 5:1–12, 21–26, 43–48; 26:36–56; Luke 11:1–4; John 18:28–40; 2 Corinthians 10:3–4; Ephesians 6:10–20; Romans 12–13;

1 Peter 3:8–17; Revelation 12:11. See also John Dear, *The Gospel of Peace: A Commentary on Matthew, Mark, and Luke from the Perspective of Nonviolence* (Orbis, 2024).

2 When I refer to the authorship of disputed canonical books such as Ephesians, 2 Timothy, Peter, etc., I do so for the sake of convenience and out of respect for tradition, not as a means of settling authorship debates. See also Boyd, *God Looks Like Jesus*, 130.

3 Contrary to popular notions, "Saul" does not become "Paul" after his conversion experience on the road to Damascus. Saul and Paul are the same person and the same name represented in the Hebrew and Roman languages, cultures in which the apostle was well versed (see, e.g., 1 Corinthians 9:19–23; Acts 22:3; Philippians 3:4–6). See Greg Lanier, "No, 'Saul the Persecutor' Did Not Become 'Paul the Apostle,'" Gospel Coalition, May 3, 2017, https://www.thegospelcoalition.org/article/no-saul-the-persecutor-did-not-become-paul-the-apostle/.

4 Jeremy Gabrielson, *Paul's Non-Violent Gospel: The Theological Politics of Peace in Paul's Life and Letters* (Pickwick Publications, 2013), 2.

5 The term "third way" was coined early in church history to distinguish Christians from the "first way" (Roman), and the "second way" (Jewish). See Gerald L. Sittser, *Resilient Faith: How the Early Christian "Third Way" Changed the World* (Brazos, 2019). This third way can be encapsulated by an anonymous second-century letter written to persuade an unbeliever named Diognetus toward Christianity, commonly called the *Epistle to Diognetus*:

> Christians cannot be distinguished from the rest of humanity by country or language or custom. They do not live in cities of their own; they do not speak a strange dialect; they do not practice an odd way of life. This teaching of theirs has not been discovered through the thinking and reflection of inquisitive people, nor do they promote any human doctrine like some people do. Although they live in Greek and non-Greek cities, as each one's lot was cast, and follow local customs in dress and diet and the rest of daily life, they also exhibit the remarkable and admittedly peculiar nature of their own citizenship. They live in their own countries, but still as foreigners. They participate as citizens in everything, but endure everything as strangers. Every foreign land is their home country, and every home country is a foreign land. They marry like everyone else and have children, but they do not throw away their offspring. They share their food table, but not their marriage bed. They happen to be in the flesh, but they do not live according to the flesh. They spend time on earth, but their citizenship is in heaven. They obey the laws that have been laid down, yet in their personal lives they surmount the law. They love everyone, but are persecuted by everyone. They are unknown, but get condemned. They are killed, yet they live. They are poor, but make many rich. They are needy in everything, yet in everything they have a surplus. They are dishonored, yet in their dishonor they receive honor. They are slandered, but they are justified. They are cursed, but they bless. They

are insulted, but they show respect. Though they do good, they get punished as evildoers. Though they are punished, they rejoice as though being brought to life. They are attacked as foreigners by Jews, and they are persecuted by Greeks, yet those who hate them have no cause for their antagonism. (*Epistle to Diognetus* 5:1–17)

6 Gabrielson, *Paul's Non-Violent Gospel*, 168–69.

7 This theme appears consistently throughout the narrative of the Bible: that God sovereignly rules over the nations and empires of humanity (e.g., Pharaoh, Nebuchadnezzar, Xerxes, Artaxerxes, Pilate) for his purposes and will.

8 I have no desire here to parse out exactly *which* ways Christians can participate in governmental systems—except to point out the clear call of the New Testament for all Christians, as aliens and foreigners whose truest citizenship is to God, to submit to their governing authorities (when not in violation of God's kingdom), to pay taxes, and to pray for *all* leaders, that there may be peace (Philippians 3:20; Romans 13:1–5; 1 Peter 2:11- 25; Romans 13:6–7; Matthew 22:15–22; 1 Timothy 2:1–3).

9 See Stanley Hauerwas, *Resident Aliens: Life in the Christian Colony*, expanded 25th ann. ed. (Abingdon Press, 2014).

10 Apocalypse, as Revelation is also known, "is the English [transliteration] of the first Greek word that occurs in the book (*apokalypsis*), meaning 'revelation.' It does not mean 'destruction,' 'end of the world,' or anything similar." Michael J. Gorman, *Reading Revelation Responsibly: Uncivil Worship and Witness, Following the Lamb into the New Creation* (Cascade Books, 2011), xi. See also Scot McKnight, *Revelation for the Rest of Us: A Prophetic Call to Follow Jesus as a Dissident Disciple* (Zondervan, 2023), 255–56; and Jeremy Duncan, *Upside-Down Apocalypse: Grounding Revelation in the Gospel of Peace* (Herald Press, 2022), 29–43.

11 Richard Bauckham, *The Theology of the Book of Revelation* (Cambridge University Press, 1993), 152.

12 Gorman, *Reading Revelation Responsibly*, 102.

13 Duncan, *Upside-Down Apocalypse*, 83.

14 Bauckham, *Theology of Revelation*, 156.

Chapter 5

1 I am using the concept of the sanctity of life in its traditional sense, not simply a political one. This is the conviction that every human being is made in the image of God (*imago Dei*) and has intrinsic value and meaning and is to be treated as such. "Human life is sacred: this means that God has consecrated each and every human being—without exception and in all circumstances—as a unique, incalculably precious being of elevated status and dignity." David Gushee, *Sacredness of Human Life: Why an Ancient Biblical Vision Is Key to the World's Future* (Eerdmans, 2013), 33.

2 For a brief introduction see J. B. Lightfoot, *The Apostolic Fathers* (Apocryphile Press, 2004). For the full translations of the original documents see Alexander Roberts and James Donaldson, eds., *Ante-Nicene Fathers*, vol. 1–10 (originally published by T. & T. Clark).

3 Gerald L. Sittser, *Resilient Faith: How the Early Christian "Third Way" Changed the World* (Brazos, 2019), 101.
4 Lisa Sowle Cahill, *Blessed Are the Peacemakers: Pacifism, Just War, and Peacebuilding* (Fortress Press, 2019), 89. Cahill notes that early Christian leaders faced tensions about the role of the nonviolent Christian as it pertained to their citizenship in the world. "Early Christian writers do not systematically analyze the nature of the moral dilemma involved in being both a Christian and a citizen, a stakeholder in the common good who benefits from the stability government provides. . . . Given the tension between the duty toward government and the common good, on the one side, and the duty not to kill, on the other, the balance is struck in favor of the Christian duty not to kill" (89–90).
5 Alan Kreider, *The Patient Ferment of the Early Church: The Improbable Rise of Christianity in the Roman Empire* (Baker Academic, 2016), 258.
6 Eli S. McCarthy, "Religious Warrants: Virtue, Nonviolence, and Just Peace," in *The Wiley Blackwell Companion to Religion and Peace*, ed. Joly-on Mitchell, Suzanna R. Millar, Francesca Po, and Martyn Percy (John Wiley & Sons, 2022), 429.
7 Roland H. Bainton, *Christian Attitudes toward War and Peace* (Abington, 1960), 66. As I discuss in the section on common ethical questions about Christian nonviolence, pacifism is distinct from passivism. Pacifism, which is often related to opposing war or having an attitude of nonresis-tance, stems from words that mean "peace-making" This is different from being passive, where someone permits things to happen and does not act.
8 Tom A. Jones, *The Kingdom of God*, vol. 3, *Learning War No More* (Illumination Publishers, 2020), 61.
9 Donald F. Durnbaugh, *The Believers' Church: The History and Character of Radical Protestantism* (Macmillan, 1968), 254.
10 Larry W. Hurtado, *Destroyer of the Gods: Early Christian Distinctiveness in the Roman World* (Baylor University Press, 2016), 152.
11 For excellent resources of primary sources, see George Kalantzis, *Caesar and the Lamb: Early Christian Attitudes on War and Military Service* (Cascade Books, 2012), 72–195; and Jean-Michael Hornus, *It Is Not Lawful for Me to Fight: Early Christian Attitudes toward War, Violence, and the State* (Wipf & Stock, 2009), 327–42.
12 Justin Martyr, *Second Apology*, chap. 12, in *Ante-Nicene Fathers*, vol. 1, 190.
13 Irenaeus, *Against Heresies*, 4.34.4, in *Ante-Nicene Fathers*, vol. 1, 512.
14 Tertullian, *De Idololatria*, trans. J. H. Wasnick and J. C. M. van Winden. Supplements to Vigliae Christianae 1 (Brill, 1987), 61.
15 Origen, *Contra Celsum*, trans. Henry Chadwick (Cambridge University Press, 1993), 290.
16 Origen, *Contra*, 133.
17 Cyprian, *Epistle 61*, §1, in *Ante-Nicene Fathers*, vol. 5, 353.
18 Cyprian, *Ad Donatum*, chap. 6, in *Ante-Nicene Fathers*, vol. 5, 276.
19 After the conversion of Constantine, Lactantius seemed to change his view considerably. Lactantius, *Divine Institutes*, 6.20, in *Ante-Nicene Fathers*, vol. 7, 187.

20 Kreider, *Patient Ferment*, 19.
21 See Kreider, *Patient Ferment*, 254.
22 Eberhard Arnold, ed., *The Early Christians in Their Own Words* (Plough Publishing, 1997), 90.
23 Notably, members of the early church didn't have options available as we do today such as medics, chaplains, and conscientious objectors, who can relinquish their obligations to violence while still serving in the military or in alternative service to the military. Many of these options are available today because of the work of Christian pacifists.
24 Ronald J. Sider, ed., *The Early Church on Killing: A Comprehensive Sourcebook on War, Abortion, and Capital Punishment* (Baker Academic, 2012), 168.
25 Michael J. Gorman, *Abortion and the Early Church: Christian, Jewish and Pagan Attitudes in the Greco-Roman World* (Wipf & Stock, 1998), 54.
26 Gorman, *Abortion and the Early Church*, 14–18. Though some first-century abortions were performed for medically therapeutic reasons for the health of the mother, first-century physicians did not have the ability to recognize and diagnose rare medical edge cases, such as anencephaly, as we do today—which only make ethical, moral, and faithful choices more nuanced and complicated surrounding abortion.
27 Rob Arner, *Consistently Pro-Life: The Ethics of Bloodshed in Ancient Christianity* (Pickwick, 2010), 56.
28 Tertullian, *Apology* 9, in *Ante-Nicene Fathers*, vol. 3, 25.
29 Eusebius of Caesarea, *Ecclesiastical History* 9.8.2, 13–15, in *Nicene and Post-Nicene Fathers*, Second Series, vol. 1, ed. Philip Schaff and Henry Wace (Christian Literature Publishing, 1890), 174–76.
30 Hippolytus, *Apostolic Tradition*, chap. 16, in *The Apostolic Tradition: A Commentary*, ed. Paul F. Bradshaw, Maxwell E. Johnson, and L. Edward Phillips (Fortress Press, 2002), 121. See also Helen Rhee, "Helen Rhee on Illness, Pain, and Health Care in Early Christianity," Calvin Institute of Christian Worship, October 25, 2024, https://worship.calvin.edu/resources/articles/helen-rhee-illness-pain-and-health-care-early-christianity.
31 Timothy S. Miller, "Basil's House of Healing," Christian History Institute, 2011, https://christianhistoryinstitute.org/magazine/article/basils-house-of-healing. See also James McCarty, Justin Bronson Barringer, and Matthew Tapie, eds., *The Business of War: Theological and Ethical Reflections on the Military-Industrial Complex* (Cascade Books, 2020), vii.

Chapter 6

1 Constantine reportedly had a vision in which he claimed to have seen a cross in the sky with the words *In hoc signo vinces* (By this sign conquer), and shortly after the vision won the Battle of Milvian Bridge, leading to the Edict of Milan and ending Christian persecution throughout the Roman Empire. "Constantine's spiritual condition has become one of the most disputed topics among historians." Jean-Michael Hornus, *It Is Not Lawful for Me to Fight: Early Christian Attitudes toward War, Violence, and the State* (Wipf & Stock, 2009), 200.

2 W. H. C. Frend, *The Early Church* (Fortress Press, 1982), 137.

3 Ronald J. Sider, ed., *The Early Church on Killing: A Comprehensive Sourcebook on War, Abortion, and Capital Punishment* (Baker Academic, 2012), 168, 190.

4 Though a few early church writings refer to Christians serving in the Roman military, the church was predominantly, if not *uniformly*, opposed to military service and all forms of violence. While certain authors mention Christians serving in the military, no early Christian author *defends* Christians serving in the military or engaging in any other kind of violence. For more, see Greg Boyd, "Was the Early Church Pacifistic? A Response to Paul Copan," Jesus Peace Collective, January 11, 2018, https://www.jesuspeacecollective.com/post/was-the-early-church-pacifistic-a-response-to-paul-copan.

5 Louis J. Swift, *The Early Fathers on War and Military Service* (Michael Glazier, 1983), 80.

6 Tom A. Jones, *The Kingdom of God*, vol. 3, *Learning War No More* (Illumination Publishers, 2020), vol. 3, 75.

7 Miranda Zapor Cruz, *Faithful Politics: Ten Approaches to Christian Citizenship and Why It Matters* (IVP Academic, 2024), 5.

8 For example, Augustine wrote:

> The divine authority itself, however, did make certain exceptions to the rule that it is against the law to kill a human being. But these exceptions include only those whom God orders to be killed, either by a law he provided or by an express command applying to a particular person at a particular time. In addition, the one who owes this service to his commander does not himself kill; rather he is, like a sword, an instrument in the user's hand. Consequently, those who, by God's authority, have waged wars have in no way acted against the commandment which says, You shall not kill; nor have those who, bearing the public power in their own person, have punished the wicked with death according to his laws, that is, according to the authority of the supremely just reason. (Augustine of Hippo, *City of God,* trans. Marcus Dods, Grapevine Books, Kindle Edition, 2025, Book I, chap. 21.)

9 Most American Christians I speak with today are the exact opposite of Augustine, in that they more readily see the problems of a Christian killing at the order of the state but have more difficulty when it comes to self-defense and the "murderer at the door" scenario.

10 When I utilize the term "two-kingdom," this is how I envision it, although historically "two-kingdom" has indicated that the Christian operates differently, even contradictorily, in private and public life, à la Augustine.

11 Eric Patterson, "A Just War View: Christian Approaches to War, Peace, and Security," in *War, Peace, and Violence: Four Christian Views*, ed. Paul Copan (InterVarsity Press, 2022), 17.

12 Just war theory considers issues surrounding (1) just cause, (2) right authority, (3) last resort, (4) proportionality, (5) probability of success, and (6) right intention. Patterson, "Just War View," 4.

13 Many of the modern Western just war writings have come from theologians who lived during the two great world wars of the early twentieth century. None of us can escape our cultural contexts and lived theologies. For a Christian pacifist's dialogue with Reinhold Niebuhr's Christian realism, see John Howard Yoder, "Reinhold Niebuhr and Christian Pacifism," *Mennonite Quarterly Review* 29 (April 1955).

John Howard Yoder was a prolific Anabaptist theologian who has perhaps had more influence than any other on the subject of Christian pacifism and nonviolence in America in the twentieth century. Despite being a towering writer in the fields of theology and ethics, Yoder failed mightily in upholding and embodying his own nonviolence theology and ethic as he perpetrated sexual violence and abuse upon women for many years. See, e.g., Rachel Waltner Goossen, "'Defanging the Beast': Mennonite Responses to John Howard Yoder's Sexual Abuse," *Mennonite Quarterly Review* 89, no. 1 (January 2015). My prayer is that we all may humbly and continually repent as we trust in the grace of God with our theologies consistently embodied—renouncing secret and shameful ways and embodying virtue (2 Corinthians 4:2).

14 Patterson, *Just War View*, 21.

15 Dorothy A. Lee, *The Ministry of Women in the New Testament: Reclaiming the Biblical Vision for Church Leadership* (Baker Academic, 2021), 12.

16 Theodore J. Koontz and Andy Alexis-Baker, eds., *Christian Attitudes to War, Peace, and Revolution: John Howard Yoder* (Brazos Press, 2009), 58.

17 Koontz, *Christian Attitudes to War*, 59–60.

18 The Donatists were a schismatic Christian sect that emerged in North Africa in the fourth century, primarily due to disagreements over the validity of sacraments administered by clergy who had apostatized during persecution.

19 Koontz, *Christian Attitudes to War*, 59.

20 George Kalantzis, *Caesar and the Lamb: Early Christian Attitudes on War and Military Service* (Cascade Books, 2012), 198.

21 Gerald L. Sittser, *Resilient Faith: How the Early Christian "Third Way" Changed the World* (Brazos, 2019), 168–169.

22 For an excellent introduction to the desert fathers and mothers, see William Harmless, *Desert Christians: An Introduction to the Literature of Early Monasticism* (Oxford University Press, 2004).

23 Kalantzis, *Caesar and the Lamb*, 199.

24 Though matters of political theology are outside the scope of this work, for helpful introductions, see Nilay Saiya, *The Global Politics of Jesus: A Christian Case for Church-State Separation* (Oxford University Press, 2022); Nathan E. Yoder, ed., *Exiles in the Empire: Believers Church Perspectives on Politics* (Pandora Press, 2006); Miranda Zapor Cruz, *Faithful Politics: Ten Approaches to Christian Citizenship and Why It Matters* (IVP Academic, 2024); and Michael Burns, *Escaping the Beast: Politics, Allegiance, and Kingdom* (Illumination Publishers, 2020).

Chapter 7

1 Indulgences were a common practice of the Catholic Church through the Middle Ages that sold remission of the temporal punishment in purgatory still due for sins after absolution.

2 "If you see that there is a lack of hangmen, constables, judges. . . and you fail to act, then you have sinned. . . . For the sword is commanded for the sake of your neighbor." Martin Luther, *Temporal Authority: To What Extent It Should Be Obeyed*, in *Luther's Works*, vol. 45, *Christian in Society II*, ed. Walther I. Brandt (Fortress Press, 1962), 81–129. Luther also said, "A soldier's work is a good and God-pleasing vocation, just as much as the work of a preacher, because it is God's work." Martin Luther, *Whether Soldiers, Too, Can Be Saved*, in *Luther's Works*, vol. 46, *The Christian in Society III*, ed. Robert C. Schultz (Fortress Press, 1967), 89–137.

3 In a papal inquisition, eighty Waldenses were burned alive for heresy in Strasbourg, France, as early as 1211 CE because they would not recognize the prerogatives of local bishops over the content of their preaching, nor to recognize standards about who was fit to preach.

4 Henry Charles Lea, *A History of the Inquisition of the Middle Ages* (Macmillan, 1906), 81.

5 For an excellent introduction, see Troy Osborne, *Radicals and Reformers: A Survey of Global Anabaptist History* (Herald Press, 2024).

6 Donald B. Kraybill, *Concise Encyclopedia of Amish, Brethren, Hutterites, and Mennonites* (Johns Hopkins University Press, 2010), xiv.

7 Stuart Murray, *The New Anabaptists: Practices for Emerging Communities* (Herald Press, 2024), 56. See also James M. Stayer, *Anabaptists and the Sword* (Wipf & Stock, 2002).

8 Alan Kreider, "Tongue Screws and Testimony," *Missio Dei* 16 (Mennonite Mission Network, 2008).

9 Jan Luyken, *Dirk Willems Rescues His Pursuer from the Ice*, engraving, in Thieleman J. van Braght, *Het Bloedig Tooneel, of Martelaers Spiegel der Doops-gesinde of Weereloose Christenen*, 2nd ed. (Hieronymus Sweerts et al., 1685).

10 See Thieleman J. van Bragt, *Martyrs Mirror: The Story of Seventeen Centuries of Christian Martyrdom from the Time of Christ to A.D. 1660* (Herald Press, 1938); and Charles E. Moore, ed., *Bearing Witness: Stories of Martyrdom and Costly Discipleship* (Plough Publishing House, 2016).

11 Donald F. Durnbaugh, *The Believers' Church: The History and Character of Radical Protestantism* (Macmillan, 1968), 66.

12 Edmund Pries, *Anabaptist Oath Refusal: Basel, Bern, and Strasbourg, 1525–1538* (Pandora Press, 2023), 385.

13 Melissa Floerer-Bixler, "An Ungovernable Faith," *The Christian Century*, February 28, 2025, https://www.christiancentury.org/voices/ungovernable-faith.

14 See John Woolman, *The Journal of John Woolman and A Plea for the Poor* (Citadel Press, 1976).

15 Stuart Murray, *The Naked Anabaptist: The Bare Essentials of a Radical Faith* (Herald Press, 2015), 196–197.

16 For more, see Donald B. Kraybill, *On the Backroad to Heaven: Old Order Hutterites, Mennonites, Amish, and Brethren* (Johns Hopkins University Press, 2002).
17 Murray, *Naked Anabaptist*, 205–207.

Chapter 8

1 Lanta Davis, *Becoming by Beholding: The Power of the Imagination in Spiritual Formation* (Baker Academic, 2024), 37–38.
2 Quoted in Gerald L. Sittser, *Resilient Faith: How the Early Christian "Third Way" Changed the World* (Brazos, 2019), 114–115.
3 Pastor Brian Zahnd calls this chapel a modern day temple to Mars, the Roman god of war. Brian Zahnd, *A Farewell to Mars: An Evangelical Pastor's Journey Toward the Biblical Gospel of Peace* (David C Cook, 2014), 178.
4 Preston Sprinkle, *Nonviolence: The Revolutionary Way of Jesus* (David C Cook, 2021), 24.
5 Andrew L. Whitehead and Samuel L. Perry, *Taking America Back for God: Christian Nationalism in the United States,* updated ed. (Oxford University Press, 2020), 10.
6 Anthea Butler, *White Evangelical Racism: The Politics of Morality in America*, 2nd ed. (University of North Carolina Press, 2021), xii.
7 Drew J. Strait, *Strange Worship: Six Steps for Challenging Christian Nationalism* (Cascade Books, 2024), 30.
8 Christopher B. Hays and C. L. Crouch, eds., *God and Guns: The Bible against American Gun Culture* (Westminster Knox Press, 2021), 4.
9 Paul D. Miller, *The Religion of American Greatness: What's Wrong with Christian Nationalism* (IVP Academic, 2022), 7.
10 Richard T. Hughes, *Christian America and the Kingdom of God* (University of Illinois Press, 2009), 24.
11 John Gast, *American Progress*, Library of Congress, https://www.loc.gov/pictures/item/97507547.
12 The Doctrine of Discovery has come under intense scrutiny and formal repudiation in the twenty-first century, including the Vatican formally rejecting it. See, e.g., Nicole Winfield, "Vatican Formally Rejects 'Doctrine of Discovery' after Indigenous Calls," PBS News, March 30, 2023, https://www.pbs.org/newshour/politics/vatican-formally-rejects-doctrine-of-discovery-after-indigenous-calls.
13 Cotton Mather, *Souldiers Counselled and Comforted: A Discourse Delivered unto Some Part of the Forces Engaged in the Just War of New-England Against the Northern & Eastern Indians, Sept. 1, 1689* (Samuel Green, 1689), 24–26.
14 Robert Alan Warrior, "Canaanites, Cowboys, and Indians: Deliverance, Conquest, and Liberation Theology Today," in *Native and Christian: Indigenous Voices on Religious Identity in the United States and Canada*, ed. James Treat (Routledge, 1996), 99, as quoted in T. Christopher Hoklotubbe (Choctaw), and H. Daniel Zacharias (Cree-Anishinaabe), "Turtle Island Biblical Interpretation," in Esau McCaulley, Janette H. Ok, Osvaldo Padilla, and Amy Peeler, eds., *The New Testament in Color:*

Multiethnic Bible Commentary (IVP Academic, 2024), 25–34.

15 Constantine R. Campbell, *Jesus v. Evangelicals: A Biblical Critique of a Wayward Movement* (Zondervan, 2023), 12.

16 Kristin Kobes Du Mez, *Jesus and John Wayne: How White Evangelicals Corrupted a Faith and Fractured a Nation* (Liveright Publishing, 2021), 4.

17 US Department of Defense, "Enlisting in the Military," Today's Military, accessed November 7, 2023, https://www.todaysmilitary.com/joining-eligibility/enlisting-military, emphasis mine.

18 As a member of the historic majority, I have never feared for my safety or feared threat from authority, even when I was on the wrong side of the law. Such is not the case for the ethnic minority experience in America.

19 Mark Weldon Whitten, *The Myth of Christian America: What You Need to Know about the Separation of Church and State* (Smyth & Helwys Publishing, 1999), 37.

20 Quoted in Stanley Hauerwas, *War and the American Difference: Theological Reflections of Violence and National Identity* (Baker Academic, 2011), 80.

21 Michael Burns, *Escaping the Beast: Politics, Allegiance, and Kingdom* (Illumination Publishers, 2020), 313.

22 For instance, Father George Zabelka was the Catholic chaplain for the 509th Composite Group—the atomic bomb group—stationed on Tinian Island. He later lamented that he had "brainwashed" the pilots by telling them they were doing God's work when they dropped a bomb on Nagasaki (directly above the largest Christian church in the Far East—killing three orders of Catholic nuns instantly). Later, Father Zabelka devoted his life to promoting Christian nonviolence and confessed, "I, like the Catholic pilot of the Nagasaki plane, was heir to a Christianity that had for 1,700 years engaged in revenge, murder, torture, the pursuit of power and prerogative and violence, all in the name of our Lord. One would have thought that I, as a priest, would have spoken out against the atomic bombing of nuns. One would have thought that I would have suggested that as a minimal standard of Catholic morality, Catholics shouldn't bomb Catholic children. I didn't speak out." George Zabelka, "I Was Brainwashed," *Sojourners* 9, no. 8 (August 1980): 12–15.

23 These queries are inspired by Sprinkle, *Nonviolence*, 228.

24 The imbalance of socioeconomic representation in the military is a controversial social and political issue in the United States. However, the US Department of Defense claims that "members of the military tended to come from backgrounds that were somewhat lower in socioeconomic status than the US average, but the differences between the military and the comparison groups were relatively modest." Office of the Assistant Secretary of Defense, "Chapter 7: Socioeconomic Status in Perspective," US Department of Defense, https://prhome.defense.gov/portals/52/Documents/POPREP/poprep99/html/chapter7/c7-perspective.htm.

25 This was the case in 2009 when Scott Roeder killed Dr. George Tiller while he was in church in Wichita, Kansas, claiming he was protecting all the preborn children who were in imminent danger. Dr. Tiller had

survived a previous murder attempt by Shelly Shannon in 1993, and was wearing body armor in church the day he died. Ed Pilkington, "For Years Anti-Abortionists Tried to Stop Doctor Tiller. Finally a Bullet Did," *The Guardian*, June 1, 2009, https://www.theguardian.com/world/2009/jun/01/us-doctor-tiller-killing-abortions.

26 Rachel D. Ramer, "Christian Pacifism on the March," Christian Research Institute, June 11, 2009, updated April 12, 2023, https://www.equip.org/articles/christian-pacifism-on-the-march/.

27 Donald F. Durnbaugh, *The Believers' Church: The History and Character of Radical Protestantism* (Wipf & Stock, 2003), 255.

28 Douglas A. Foster, Paul M. Blowers, Anthony L. Dunnavant, and D. Newell William, *The Encyclopedia of the Stone-Campbell Movement* (Eerdmans, 2004), 586.

29 John Mark Hicks, ed., *Resisting Babel: Allegiance to God and the Problem of Government* (ACU Press, 2020), 106.

30 Foster et al., *Encyclopedia of Stone-Campbell*, 587.

31 Paul Alexander, *Peace to War: Shifting Allegiances in the Assemblies of God* (Cascadia, 2009).

32 Foster et al., *Encyclopedia of Stone-Campbell*, 586.

33 For instance, some exceptions were "the radical noncooperation tactics of Corbett Bishop, a member of the Manhattan, New York, Church of Christ, [who] influenced the nonviolent protest techniques of the peace and civil rights movements." Foster, *Encyclopedia of Stone-Campbell*, 587.

34 Foster, *Encyclopedia of Stone-Campbell*, 587. See also Johnnie Collins, "Pacifism in the Churches of Christ: 1866–1945" (doctoral diss., Middle Tennessee State University, 1978).

35 Their name "was the battle cry of English soldiers willing to lay down their lives for their king and their country. And now it has become our mission, to lay down our lives for our King [Jesus] and our country." "For King & Country: From Rebecca St James sidemen to CCM success," CrossRhythms, May 23, 2012, https://www.crossrhythms.co.uk/articles/music/For_King__Country_From_Rebecca_St_James_sidemen_to_CCM_success_/48617/p1/.

36 Du Mez, *Jesus and John* Wayne, 5.

37 Chris Cameron, "These Are the People Who Died in Connection with the Capitol Riot," *The New York Times*, January 5, 2022, https://www.nytimes.com/2022/01/05/us/politics/jan-6-capitol-deaths.html.

38 Associated Press, "Christianity on Display at Capitol Riot Sparks New Debate," AP News, January 28, 2021, https://apnews.com/article/christianity-capitol-riot-6f13ef0030ad7b5a6f37a1e3b7b4c898.

39 Both quoted in Campbell, *Jesus v. Evangelicals*, 1.

40 Melissa Florer-Bixler, "Anabaptist Trumpism," *The Leavings*, January 29, 2025, https://melissaflorerbixler.substack.com/p/anabaptist-trumpism. I deal further with the issue of policing and Christian pacifism in Common Ethical Questions about Christian Nonviolence.

Chapter 9

1 Craig M. Watts, *Disciple of Peace: Alexander Campbell on Pacifism, Violence, and the State* (Doulos Christou Press, 2005), 121.

2 See Miroslav Volf and Ryan McAnnaly-Linz, *Public Faith in Action: How to Think Carefully, Engage Wisely, and Vote with Integrity* (Brazos Press, 2017), 118.

3 Barak Obama, "Remarks by the President on Osama Bin Laden," Obama White House Archives, May 2, 2011, https://obamawhitehouse.archives.gov/blog/2011/05/02/osama-bin-laden-dead, emphasis mine.

4 Wink references the *Enuma Elish*, the Babylonian creation myth from around 1250 BCE that tells the story of the creation of the world being born from violence and destruction from the gods, a text that the Genesis creation account is clearly in conversation with. Walter Wink, *The Powers That Be: Theology for a New Millennium* (Galilee, 1999), 44.

5 Wink, *The Powers That Be*, 48.

6 Donald J. Trump, "Patriot Day 2025, The 24th Anniversary of the September 11 Terrorist Attacks," The White House, Presidential Actions, September 11, 2025, https://www.whitehouse.gov/presidential-actions/2025/09/patriot-day-2025-the-24th-annivresary-of-the-september-11-terrorist-attacks/.

7 Quoted in Wink, *The Powers That Be*, 52.

8 Writing in the late 1990s, Wink says that viewer interest determines most television and movie programming. "Film producers provide what the ratings tell them will generate the most profit. . . . By making violence pleasurable, fascinating, and entertaining, the Powers are able to delude people into compliance with a system that is cheating them of their very lives." Wink, *The Powers That Be*, 53.

9 Preston Sprinkle, "The Only Way to Stop a Bad Guy with a Gun, Is a Good Guy with a Gun," Theology in the Raw, April 27, 2016, https://theologyintheraw.com/the-only-way-to-stop-a-bad-guy-with-a-gun-is-a-good-guy-with-a-gun/.

10 For instance see the FBI report on the 160 active shooter incidents between 2000–2013: "A Study of Active Shooter Incidents in the United States Between 2000 and 2013," Federal Bureau of Investigation, accessed May 30, 2025, https://www.fbi.gov/file-repository/reports-and-publications/active-shooter-study-2000-2013-1.pdf/view.

11 Timothy O'Brien, *The Things They Carried* (Houghton Mifflin, 1990), 68–69.

12 Joan Benach and Carles Muntaner, "Arms, Conventional Wisdom, and Public Health Prevention," *International Journal of Health Services* 53, no. 1 (January 2023): 69–73, https://doi.org/10.1177/00207314221125057. See also Nicholas Kristof, "More Americans Killed by Guns since 1968 Than in All US Wars," PolitiFact, August 27, 2015, https://www.politifact.com/factchecks/2015/aug/27/nicholas-kristof/more-americans-killed-guns-1968-all-wars-says-colu/.

13 Shane Claiborne and Michael Martin, *Beating Guns: Hope for People Who Are Weary of Violence* (Brazos Press, 2019), 190–191.

14 The story of Samson is told as a tragedy in the book of Judges. A man with a powerful gifting from God who does not use it for God's glory. Samson breaks his Nazirite vows, has sex with foreign women, doesn't deliver the Israelites from oppression, and only seems to have faith in God in the final moments of his life, blinded and under captivity. See K. Lawson Younger Jr., "Introduction to Judges," in *NIV Biblical Theology Study Bible*, ed. D. A. Carson (Zondervan, 2018), 384–92.
15 Christopher B. Hays, "'Do Not Be Afraid': The Walls of Jerusalem and the Guns of America," in Christopher B. Hays and C. L. Crouch, eds., *God and Guns: The Bible against American Gun Culture* (Westminster Knox Press, 2021), 57–58.
16 Cited in Eric A. Seibert, *Disarming the Church: Why Christians Must Forsake Violence to Follow Jesus and Change the World* (Cascade Books, 2018), 19.
17 James E. Atwood, *Collateral Damage: Changing the Conversation about Firearms and Faith* (Herald Press, 2019), 17.
18 Christopher B. Hays, "Gun Violence in America: A Theological Treatment for a Deadly Epidemic," in Hays and Crouch, eds., *God and Guns*, 1.
19 The Second Amendment of the US Constitution reads, "A well-regulated Militia, being necessary to the security of a free State, the right of the people to keep and bear Arms, shall not be infringed." Library of Congress, "Second Amendment," https://constitution.congress.gov/constitution/amendment-2/.
20 Claiborne and Martin, *Beating Guns*, 150–51.
21 Associated Press, "Hundreds Gather at Church for Blessing Ceremony Featuring AR-15s," CBS News, last modified February 28, 2018, https://www.cbsnews.com/news/hundreds-of-worshipers-gather-at-church-hosting-ceremony-featuring-ar-15s/.
22 Nilay Saiya, *The Global Politics of Jesus: A Christian Case for Church-State Separation* (Oxford University Press, 2022), 250.
23 René Girard, trans. James G. Williams, *I See Satan Fall Like Lightning* (Orbis, 2001), xviii.
24 John Berkman and Michael Cartwright, eds., *The Hauerwas Reader: Stanley Hauerwas* (Duke University Press, 2001), 320.
25 Hays and Crouch, *God and Guns*, 23–24 (emphasis original).
26 Lt. Col. Dave Grossman and Gloria DeGaetano, *Stop Teaching Our Kids to Kill: A Call to Action Against TV, Movie, and Video Game Violence*, revised and updated ed. (Harmony Books, 2014), 8, Kindle. See also Grossman, *On Killing: The Psychological Cost of Learning to Kill in War and Society* (Back Bay Books, 2009).
27 B. Joseph, H. Hosseinpour, and J. Sakran, "Defining the Problem: 53 Years of Firearm Violence Afflicting America's Schools," *Journal of American College of Surgeons*, March 6, 2024, https://www.facs.org/media-center/press-releases/2024/study-quantifies-dramatic-rise-in-school-shootings-and-related-fatalities-since-1970.
28 See Michael L. Budde, *Foolishness to Gentiles: Essays on Empire, Nationalism, and Discipleship* (Cascade Books, 2022), 174.

Chapter 10

1 In our congregation of about a hundred, those who chose to participate in the research took an opening anonymous online survey before the series (53 people) and a closing anonymous online survey after the series (36 people). I conducted personal interviews with nine participants who took both the opening and closing surveys and participated in at least two of the three small group discussions. The personal interview respondents ranged in age from twenty-nine to seventy-one. They included both males and females who self-identified as White, Black, African American, Chinese, and Asian. Only one of the interview participants was in the small group leader training the year prior when I guided them through Tom A. Jones, *The Kingdom of God*, vol. 3, *Learning War No More* (Illumination Publishers, 2020).

2 For example see "Book Recommendations," Jesus Peace Collective, https://www.jesuspeacecollective.com/post/book-recommendations.

3 With their permission, I use single-name pseudonyms to protect individuals' privacy throughout this chapter.

4 See Christopher B. Hays, "'Do Not Be Afraid': The Walls of Jerusalem and the Guns of America," in Christopher B. Hays and C. L. Crouch, eds., *God and Guns: The Bible against American Gun Culture* (Westminster Knox Press, 2021), 75.

5 This popular phrase was coined in the Albigensian Crusade of the thirteenth century, where "both church and town were looted, and the inhabitants massacred, with clerics, women, and children being killed inside the churches. . . . Arnald-Amalric is said to have been asked how the attackers should distinguish between heretic and Catholic, to which he replied, *Caedite eos. Novit enim Dominus qui sunt eis*—'kill them all, God will know his own.'" Caesarius of Heisterbach: vol. II, 296–98, as quoted in Michael Costen, *The Cathars and the Albigensian Crusade* (Manchester University Press, 1997), 123.

6 Preston Sprinkle, "The Killer at The Door," *Theology in the Raw*, May 2, 2016, https://theologyintheraw.com/the-killer-at-the-door/.

7 See Marie Dennis, ed., *Choosing Peace: The Catholic Church Returns to Gospel Nonviolence* (Orbis, 2018); and the websites of Pax Christi International and Jesus Peace Collective.

8 In 2023 in the United States, "guns were the leading cause of death among children & teens (ages 1–17), accounting for more deaths than car crashes, overdoses, or cancers." While "Black youth face alarmingly high rates of gun violence. More than half (55%) of all Black older teens (ages 15–17) who died in 2022 were killed by a gun." In 2023, the highest number of people ever recorded died by gun suicide, with nearly six out of every ten gun deaths being suicides in the US. S. Villarreal et al., "Gun Violence in the United States 2022: Examining the Burden among Children and Teens," Johns Hopkins Center for Gun Violence Solutions, accessed September 13, 2024, https://publichealth.jhu.edu/center-for-gun-violence-solutions/annual-firearm-violence-data. "Gun Violence in the United States 2023: Examining the Gun Suicide Epidemic," Johns Hopkins Center

for Gun Violence Solutions, June 2025, https://publichealth.jhu.edu/sites/default/files/2025-06/2023-cgvs-gun-violence-in-the-united-states.pdf.

Chapter 11

1 Michael J. Gorman, *Reading Revelation Responsibly: Uncivil Worship and Witness, Following the Lamb into the New Creation* (Cascade Books, 2011), 55.

2 Ronald J. Sider, *Nonviolent Action: What Christian Ethics Demands but Most Christians Have Never Really Tried* (Brazos Press, 2015), 3.

3 Carl R. Trueman, *The Rise and Triumph of the Modern Self: Cultural Amnesia, Expressive Individualism, and the Road to Sexual Revolution* (Crossway, 2020), 85–88. See also Alasdair MacIntyre, *After Virtue: A Study in Moral Theory*, 2nd ed. (Duckworth, 1985).

4 For more on Christian cultural engagement, see Gerald L. Sittser, *Resilient Faith: How the Early Christian "Third Way" Changed the World* (Brazos, 2019); Stephen O. Presley, *Cultural Sanctification: Engaging the World Like the Early Church* (Eerdmans, 2024); Michael Green, *Evangelism in the Early Church*, rev. ed. (Eerdmans, 2003), Rod Dreher, *The Benedict Option: A Strategy for Christians in a Post-Christian Nation* (Sentinel, 2017); and Trueman, *Rise and Triumph of the Modern Self.*

5 Dietrich Bonhoeffer, *The Cost of Discipleship* (SCM Press, 1959), 144–45.

6 Lisa Sowle Cahill, *Blessed Are the Peacemakers: Pacifism, Just War, and Peacebuilding* (Fortress Press, 2019), 330.

7 See Stephen O. Presley, *Cultural Sanctification: Engaging the World Like the Early Church* (Eerdmans, 2024).

8 Vince Bantu, *A Multitude of All Peoples: Engaging Ancient Christianity's Global Identity* (IVP Academic, 2020), 229.

9 Presley, *Cultural Sanctification*, 12.

10 "Pacifists, and their *a priori* rejection of violence, presume universal divine favor upon their act, and in doing so, only oppose one principality (war) by participating in another (ideological pacifism)." Myles Werntz, *Bodies of Peace: Ecclesiology, Nonviolence, and Witness* (Fortress Press, 2014), 163.

11 Sider, *Nonviolent Action*, 158.

12 Harriet Bicksler, "Teaching Peace to Children Who Play War," in *A Peace Reader*, E. Morris Sider and Luke Keefer Jr., eds. (Evangel Publishing House, 2002), 130–139. For an excellent resource to help introduce the ways of peace in the Scriptures to children, see *The Peace Table: A Storybook Bible* (Herald Press, 2023).

13 For examples of this, see Sider, *A Peace Reader*; and Shawn Graves and Marlena Graves, eds., *The Gospel of Peace in a Violent World: Christian Nonviolence for Communal Flourishing* (IVP Academic, 2022).

14 Shane Claiborne and Michael Martin, *Beating Guns: Hope for People Who Are Weary of Violence* (Brazos Press, 2019).

15 Graves and Graves, *Gospel of Peace*, 125.

16 Martin Luther King Jr., "Martin Luther King, Jr.—Acceptance Speech," NobelPrize.org, 1964, accessed November 22, 2025, https://www.nobelprize.org/prizes/peace/1964/king/acceptance-speech/.

17 For the differences between unjust and just peacemaking, see Glen H. Stassen, ed., *Just Peacemaking: The New Paradigm for the Ethics of Peace and War*, new ed. (Pilgrim Press, 2008).
18 See Marie Fortune, *Sexual Violence: The Unmentionable Sin* (Pilgrim Press, 1983); and *Sexual Violence: The Sin Revisited* (Pilgrim Press, 2005).
19 David C. Cramer and Myles Werntz, *A Field Guide to Christian Nonviolence: Key Thinkers, Activists, and Movements for the Gospel of Peace* (Baker Academic, 2022), 128.
20 Laura Kiesel, "Don't Blame Mental Illness for Mass Shootings; Blame Men," *Politico*, January 17, 2018, https://www.politico.com/magazine/story/2018/01/17/gun-violence-masculinity-216321; Frank T. Andrew, "'If You Give a Man a Gun': The Evolutionary Psychology of Mass Shootings," *The Conversation*, December 4, 2015, https://theconversation.com/if-you-give-a-man-a-gun-the-evolutionary-psychology-of-mass-shootings-51782.
21 Claiborne and Martin, *Beating Guns*, 130.
22 Lauren F. Winner, "Magnolia Trees and Cardigan Sweaters: Unexpected Metaphors for God," TheoEd Talks, April 2, 2019, https://youtu.be/BBolByb6xmA.
23 Claiborne and Martin, *Beating Guns*, 130.
24 Monica A. Coleman, *Making a Way Out of No Way: A Womanist Theology* (Fortress Press, 2008), 31.
25 Walter Wink, *Violence and Nonviolence in South Africa: Jesus' Third Way* (New Society, 1987), 34.
26 *Characktēr*: where we get our word *character* in English, literally means the instrument used for engraving or carving, the mark stamped upon an instrument, the exact expression (the image) of any person or thing.
27 William James, "The Moral Equivalent of War," in William James, *The Moral Equivalent of War, and Other Essays*, ed. John K. Roth (Harper & Row, 1971), 3. Interestingly, this essay originally appeared in 1910, before the two world wars.
28 Cahill, *Blessed Are the Peacemakers*, 325–26.
29 Martin Luther King Jr., "Acceptance Speech," https://www.nobelprize.org/prizes/peace/1964/king/acceptance-speech/.

Common Scriptural Questions about Christian Nonviolence

1 See Jesus Peace Collective, https://www.jesuspeacecollective.com.
2 Philip Jenkins, *Laying Down the Sword: Why We Can't Ignore the Bible's Violent Verses* (Harper Collins, 2011), 247.
3 See "US Military Weapons Inscribed with Secret 'Jesus' Bible Codes," *ABC News*, January 18, 2010, https://abcnews.go.com/Blotter/us-military-weapons-inscribed-secret-jesus-bible-codes/story?id=9575794.
4 For instance, see of Jesus (David C Cook, 2021), 235–53; Ronald J. Sider, *If Jesus Is Lord: Loving Our Enemies in an Age of Violence* (Baker Academic, 2024), 77–99; Tom A. Jones, *The Kingdom of God*, vol. 3, *Learning War No More* (Illumination Publishers, 2020), 114–63; Jason Porterfield, *Fight Like Jesus: How Jesus Waged Peace Throughout Holy Week* (Herald

Press, 2022), 41–61, 131–137; Stanley Hauerwas et al., eds., *The Wisdom of the Cross: Essays in Honor of John Howard Yoder* (Wipf & Stock, 1999), 65–68; John Howard Yoder, *What Would You Do? A Serious Answer to a Standard Question* (Herald Press, 1992); Tripp York and Justin Bronson Barringer, eds., *A Faith Not Worth Fighting For: Addressing Commonly Asked Questions about Christian Nonviolence* (Cascade Books, 2012).

5 The word translated as "sword" here is what we would consider a large dagger, not a medieval long sword.

6 "There are several ways of interpreting this difficult clause: (1) *Let the person with a purse and bag and let the one not having a purse and bag sell his cloak, and let them both go and buy a sword.* (2) *Let the person with a purse and bag take them now (whereas before he did not), and let the person not having a sword, let him sell his cloak and buy one.* This interpretation is followed by the NIV, RSV, NASB, NEB. (3) *Let the person having a sword also take a purse and bag, and the one who does not have a sword, let him sell his cloak and buy one.* The second interpretation is the most probable." Robert H. Stein, *Luke*, The New American Commentary, vol. 24 (Broadman & Holman, 1992), 555.

7 John Nolland, *Luke 18:35–24:53*, vol. 35C, Word Biblical Commentary (Word, Incorporated, 1993), 1076.

8 N. T. Wright, *Jesus and the Victory of God: Christian Origins and the Question of God*, vol. 2 (Fortress Press, 1997), 334, 416.

9 Richard B. Hays, *The Moral Vision of the New Testament: A Contemporary Introduction to New Testament Ethics* (HarperCollins Publishers, 1996), 334.

10 There is no textual evidence that Jesus uses the whip on people. See Porterfield, *Fight Like Jesus*, 50–53; Sider, *Jesus Is Lord*, 83; and Thomas R. Yoder Neufeld, *Killing Enmity: Violence and the New Testament* (Baker Academic, 2011), 60–61.

11 Timothy J. Demy and J. Daryl Charles, *War, Peace, and Christianity: Questions and Answers from a Just-War Perspective* (Crossway, 2010), 370.

12 Paul Copan and Matthew Flannagan, *Did God Really Command Genocide? Coming to Terms with the Justice of God* (Baker Books, 2014), 302.

13 Rogers Brubaker and David D. Laitin, "Ethnic and Nationalist Violence," *Annual Review of Sociology* 24 (1998): 427.

14 Andy Alexis-Baker, "What about the Centurion? A Roman Soldier's Faith and Christian Pacifism," in Tripp York and Justin Bronson Barringer, eds., *A Faith Not Worth Fighting For: Addressing Commonly Asked Questions about Christian Nonviolence* (Cascade Books, 2012), 178.

15 I am indebted to Dr. Douglas Jacoby for pointing out that "if *extortion* [taking someone's property by violence] is forbidden to soldiers (Luke 3:13), then taking *lives* would (a fortiori) [used to express a conclusion for which there is stronger evidence than for a previously accepted one] be even more prohibited" (emphasis in the original). Douglas Jacoby, email correspondence, used with permission. For more on this question, see Jones, *Kingdom of God*, vol. 3, 118–20; Sprinkle, *Nonviolence*, 244–246; Sider, *If Jesus Is Lord*, 79–82; Alexis-Baker, "What about the Centurion," 170–83.

16 For instance, it is well documented that Roman centurions often led soldiers in ritual pagan worship, which would have certainly been seen as sin (idolatry) by Jesus, the apostles, and John the Baptist. However, no mention is made in these instances of them being called to repent of their pagan worship, revealing that these passages do not aim to give an exhaustive list of repentance.

17 As you look closely at the metanarrative of the Bible, you see this theme consistently: God sovereignly rules over leaders, nations, and empires (e.g., Pharaoh, Nebuchadnezzar, Xerxes, Artaxerxes, Pilate) for his purpose and will.

18 I have no desire to parse out precisely which ways Christians *can* participate in human governmental systems, other than to note the clear call of the New Testament for all Christians, as aliens and foreigners in the world (meaning that their truest citizenship and allegiance is to God; Philippians 3:20), to submit to their governing authorities (when not in violation of God's kingdom; Romans 13:1–5; 1 Peter 2:11–25), to pay taxes (even when those taxes support evil, as they did in Jesus' and Paul's contexts; Matthew 22:15–22; Romans 13:6–7), and to pray for all leaders that there may be peace (1 Timothy 2:1–3).

19 See Scot McKnight, *Revelation for the Rest of Us: A Prophetic Call to Follow Jesus as a Dissident Disciple* (Zondervan, 2023); Jeremy Duncan, *Upside-Down Apocalypse: Grounding Revelation in the Gospel of Peace* (Herald Press, 2022); Richard Bauckham, *The Theology of the Book of Revelation* (Cambridge University Press, 1993).

20 Thomas Merton, *Opening the Bible* (Liturgical Press, 1986), 11.

21 See, e.g., Eric A. Seibert, *Disturbing Divine Behavior: Troubling Old Testament Image of God* (Fortress Press, 2009). I don't find this kind of argument persuasive, primarily because it creates as many problems as it tries to solve as it requires that the reader put themselves "over the text" when choosing what has been divinely inspired. Seibert himself says that there could be a confusion of his position with Marcion's of the second century, which he distinguishes by Marcion's rejection of the entire Old Testament as inspired, whereas Seibert only rejects parts of it. Obviously, the slippery slope is dramatically in view here. While God communicates to humanity through human involvement and agency, either divine revelation is revealed to us from outside ourselves, or it is not, and relativism is the only option. For more, see Kevin Vanhoozer, *Is There Meaning in This Text? The Bible, the Reader, and the Morality of Literary Knowledge* (Zondervan Academic, 2009); and Vanhoozer, *Mere Christian Hermeneutics: Transfiguring What It Means to Read the Bible Theologically* (Zondervan Academic, 2024).

22 See Sider, *If Jesus Is Lord*, 147–67.

23 Stuart Murray comments, "Anabaptists have been so concerned with listening to Jesus that they have often given the impression that the Old Testament is merely preparatory, not really worth engaging with on its own terms," which has "left the Anabaptist tradition with an inadequate appreciation of the Old Testament." Stuart Murray, *The Naked Anabaptist: The Bare Essentials of a Radical Faith* (Herald Press, 2015), 193–94.

24 Richard Hays, "The Future of New Testament Theology" (Inaugural Lecture to the George Washington Ivey New Testament Chair, Duke Divinity School, Durham, NC, January 28, 2003), 9, as quoted in Richard S. Hess and Elmer A. Martens, eds., *War in the Bible and Terrorism in the Twenty-First Century* (Eisenbrauns, 2008), 35.
25 Sider, *If Jesus Is Lord*, 156.
26 Hess, *War in the Bible*, 51.
27 Sider, *If Jesus Is Lord*, 167.

Common Ethical Questions about Christian Nonviolence

1 Walter Wink, *Jesus and Nonviolence: A Third Way* (Fortress Press, 2003), 102–3, emphasis mine.
2 Lisa Sowle Cahill, *Blessed Are the Peacemakers: Pacifism, Just War, and Peacebuilding* (Fortress Press, 2019), 17.
3 C. S. Lewis, *The Weight of Glory: And Other Addresses* (HarperOne, 2001), 86.
4 Ambrose, *Of the Duties of Clergy*, 1.36.179; quoted in James Turner Johnson, *Quest for Peace: Three Moral Traditions in Western Cultural History* (Princeton University Press, 1987), 55.
5 *Merriam-Webster*, s.v. "Pacifism," accessed November 8, 2023, https://www.merriam-webster.com/dictionary/pacifism.
6 Stanford Encyclopedia of Philosophy, s.v. "Pacifism," accessed November 8, 2023, https://plato.stanford.edu/entries/pacifism.
7 *Cambridge Dictionary*, s.v. "Passive," accessed November 8, 2023, https://dictionary.cambridge.org/us/dictionary/learner-english/passive.
8 As quoted in Ched Myers, *Binding the Strong Man: A Political Reading of Mark's Story of Jesus* (Orbis, 1988), 290.
9 John Howard Yoder, *What Would You Do? A Serious Answer to a Standard Question* (Herald Press, 1992), 41.
10 See also Preston Sprinkle, *Nonviolence: The Revolutionary Way of Jesus* (David C Cook, 2021), 247.
11 For a full-length treatment, see Robert Brimlow, *What about Hitler? Wrestling with Jesus's Call to Nonviolence in an Evil World* (Brazos, 2006), and the shorter summary in chapter 4 of Tripp York and Justin Bronson Barringer, eds., *A Faith Not Worth Fighting For: Addressing Commonly Asked Questions about Christian Nonviolence* (Cascade Books, 2012), 44–59.
12 Walter Wink, *Engaging the Powers: Discernment and Resistance in a World of Domination* (Fortress Press, 1992), 36.
13 There is a popular notion in American evangelicalism that Bonhoeffer is the quintessential individual who reveals the breaking point of Christian pacifism (see Eric Metaxas, *Bonhoeffer: Pastor, Martyr, Prophet, Spy* [Nelson Books, 2020] and the subsequent 2024 movie *Bonhoeffer: Pastor. Spy. Assassin*). However, scholars debate what role and activity Bonhoeffer had in the assassination plot of Hitler. See Mark Thiessen Nation, *Discipleship in a World Full of Nazis: Recovering the True Legacy of Dietrich Bonhoeffer* (Cascade Books, 2022).
14 Brimlow, "What about Hitler?," 52.

15 Though Gandhi was not explicitly a Christian to my knowledge, he did draw inspiration from Jesus and the Sermon on the Mount and often read the Gospels and other parts of the New Testament. See Dr. P. T. Subrahmanyan, "Mahatma Gandhi and the Sermon on the Mount," Gandhi Research Foundation, accessed July 14, 2025, https://www.mkgandhi.org/articles/mahatma-gandhi-and-sermon-on-the-mount.html.
16 Charles Griswold, "Forgiveness and Apology: What, When, Why?" *Tikkun* (March/April 2008): 21–26, quoted in Brimlow, "What about Hitler?" in York and Barringer, *Not Worth Fighting For*, 59.
17 Celsus quoted in Origen's reply, *Contra Celsum* 8.68; quoted in Ronald J. Sider, ed., *The Early Church on Killing: A Comprehensive Sourcebook on War, Abortion, and Capital Punishment* (Baker Academic, 2012), 80.
18 Dennis Romero and Anthony Cusumano, "Death Sentence Upheld for Dylann Roof, Who Killed 9 in South Carolina Church Shooting," NBC News, August 25, 2021, https://www.nbcnews.com/news/us-news/death-sentence-upheld-man-who-killed-9-south-carolina-church-n1277667.
19 For more, see chapter 6 in York and Barringer, *Not Worth Fighting For*, 85–106.
20 It can be argued that to expel (*exairō*) someone from the fellowship, as in 1 Corinthians 5, is an example of nonviolent "policing" in the New Testament.
21 Gerald W. Schlabach, "Must Christian Pacifists Reject Police Force?," in York and Barringer, *Not Worth Fighting For*, 61. For an insightful diagram that seeks to plot and interrelate the tensions of various understandings of Christian involvement and utilization of law enforcement, see 74ff. For inspiring examples of imaginative peaceful and nonviolent stories in the face of threat, see Dave Jackson, *Dial 911: Peaceful Christians and Urban Violence* (Herald Press, 1981).
22 Notably because of Christian pacifists, there are noncombatant and conscientious objector statuses in America that *could* allow Christian participation in varying capacities in these organizations without being required to kill. For a dramatic depiction of a true story about this, and how ridiculed these people often are, see the (violent and gruesome) 2016 movie *Hacksaw Ridge*.
23 Edward A. Malloy, *The Ethics of Law Enforcement and Criminal Punishment* (University Press of America, 1982), 17, quoted in Stanley Hauerwas et al., eds., *The Wisdom of the Cross: Essays in Honor of John Howard Yoder* (Wipf & Stock, 1999), 96.
24 John Howard Yoder, *The Original Revolution: Essays on Christian Pacifism* (Herald Press, 1977), 56, quoted in Tobias Winright, "From Police Officers to Peace Officers," in Hauerwas et al., *Wisdom of the Cross*, 109.

The Author

Jon Sherwood serves as the executive director of Asheville Church Network, a diverse micro church network in the western North Carolina region. He is also the founder of Jesus Peace Collective, an ecumenical group of like-minded Jesus followers committed to living and spreading the nonviolent, active peacemaking teachings of Jesus and the early Church. Jon is the host of the *UNpolished Church* podcast and holds a DMin in Justice and Peacemaking from Mercer University. Learn more at JonSherwood.com.